"The soul that on Jesus hath leaned for repose,
I will not, I will not desert to his foes;
That soul, though all hell should endeavor to shake,
I'll never, no, never, no, never forsake."

—HOW FIRM A FOUNDATION

15 SIMPLE STEPS

TO LOSING YOUR SALVATION

By Rick Schworer

15 Simple Steps to Losing Your Salvation

Copyright © 2011 Rick Schworer

ISBN   9781890120795

Library of Congress   2011944084

All Scripture passages in this book are taken from the Authorized King James Version, any deviations are not intentional.

Published by Daystar Publishing
Miamitown, OH 45041
www.daystarpublishing.org

Also available at www.truthandsong.com

Dedicated to my nephew, Aaron.
Melissa and I are very proud of you and hope
you continue to grow in the Lord.

Special thanks to my wife for all her help, to Laura, an amazing Canadian who can proofread like nobody's business, and Andrew, for another great book cover.

Introduction

It isn't all that unique for most Christians, especially second-generation Christians, to have doubts about their salvation every now and then. I believe this doubt comes from three sources, and the point of this book is to address all three of them.

The first is a muddied idea about how people get saved to begin with. Some feel that there's no way that God could save a sinner like them, because of what they did before salvation and some because of sin after salvation. Many second-generation Christians hear the graphic testimonies of those who were saved out of the filth of the world and it leaves them wondering if they're really saved at all. Some hear dramatic testimonies of people who were "gloriously saved" (nothing wrong with that!) and because they don't know the color of the carpet or the exact minute they were saved they feel that their salvation testimony is shallow. Any salvation testimony is a wonderful thing, be it saved out of sin or *from* sin – either way you're saved from Hell! All these sorts of doubts come from a misunderstanding of what salvation is and how it works.

The second doubt comes from thinking you can "lose it." Though no one really knows for sure which sin it is that damns saved people and which ones are okay, most Christians today think that you have to earn your salvation *after* you've trusted Christ to save you. It doesn't really make much sense, but it is what it is. Most of this book is aimed at striking down this false doctrine by showing the insurmountable tasks a person would have to accomplish to actually "un-save" themselves. Those who believe they can lose it usually have a shallow understanding of the New Testament or may have purposely ignored or twisted many of the bedrock foundational doctrines of what actually happens to a person once they trust Christ. The promises and doctrines for a child of God in the Church Age all dovetail with each other and they support the doctrine of eternal security. Eternal security is not a doctrine based upon a few verses here and there, it's not merely a table with four legs, it has at least fifteen different legs supporting it that you'd have to knock out to lose your salvation. It's a doctrine upheld by several other doctrines.

Lastly, people have doubts because they run into difficult passages from time to time. They're there, and I'm not going to pretend they're not. Throughout the whole Bible there are difficult passages; this isn't anything new to a Bible student. You can grab verses to teach that Jesus Christ has already returned, that the future resurrection is non-existent and it's merely spiritual, that there's no Heaven or Hell, and that God can sin - the list goes on and on. All these terrible things are lies. We're not going to look at every difficult passage, or at every passage that the other side throws out. I believe it to be more profitable for a person to know on their own how to understand tough passages instead of telling them what every single difficult passage means. So in the last chapter we're going to lay down a seven point checklist of things to consider when you run into a "toughie."

It's my desire for this book to be easy to read and to move quickly so as to not bog down the reader. I've done my best to make this flow quickly and smoothly because the message of assurance is very important. You'll find as you go throughout the book the doctrines and concepts become deeper and richer, whereas the beginning of the book is filled mostly with simple ideas and stand alone verses that teach eternal security. Be it milk or meat, the New Testament is abounding in the truth of eternal security.

When my wife was pregnant with our second child, it was scary for her. I assume that any mother can attest to this. She was afraid of what the child-birth experience was going to be like: the labor, the pain, the healing afterwards, the "what ifs" if things went wrong. A very sweet and wise woman told my wife these words that completely changed her mindset:

Don't let the Devil steal the joy of today because of the fear of tomorrow.

One of the most basic and fundamental needs of a Christian is to have assurance of salvation. A child of God must know he's secure in Christ and that God will always love Him. Without assurance, it's hard to do anything for the Lord and you could live your life in doubt and frustration, with all your focus on yourself. God has promised to fulfill our needs, *including assurance.*

It is my hope and prayer that this book will help give you the assurance you need to serve the Lord with joy and confidence.

Contents

Chapter One
Are You Really Saved?

"Therefore it is of faith..."

Romans 4:16

A big part of assurance comes from knowing you actually got saved right the first time. Half of the Christians who struggle with assurance of salvation already believe in eternal security – they just don't think they ever did it right to begin with. How many young people have been "re-treaded," summer camp after summer camp, because of this problem? Exasperated, one teenager said, *"If I'm not saved now, I ain't ever gonna be saved!"*

One lady spoke of how she wondered for years and years if she was really saved. She was hesitant to try and serve the Lord because she felt inadequate and unqualified, unsure if she had the power of God working within her. This lady went to church every Sunday, but she never got assurance until she sat underneath the preaching of a Bible believing church. It was learning the truth of the word of God that gave her the peace and confidence she needed.

Does anyone really think that God wants His people living their lives in doubt and worry? God is not the author of confusion, and salvation is supposed to be simple. Sometimes even the most doctrinally sound have trouble with what is supposed to be the most rudimentary belief we have!

I Cor. 14:33, "For God is not the author of confusion, but of peace, as in all churches of the saints."

II Cor. 11:3, "But I fear, lest by any means, as the serpent beguiled Eve through his subtilty, so your minds should be corrupted from the simplicity that is in Christ."

If you struggle in this area, ask yourself this question:

What am I trusting in to get me to Heaven?

If you answered (and meant from the heart), "Jesus Christ alone," then you're saved. There's nothing more to it than that. If you start arguing with yourself about whether or not you repented correctly, prayed the right words, or anything else, please understand you are making a huge mistake.

You're shifting the focus off of Jesus and onto yourself.

A man who is dying of thirst doesn't care if the water is served to him in a paper cup or a horse trough – he's dying of thirst and he needs the water. If someone offers him the water all he needs to take it is knowledge of the fact that he needs the water! All that really matters in the end is that he drank the water, not what he went through

2

before he drank it. All a man needs to be saved is knowledge of the fact that he's lost and that he needs a Saviour.

What about Repentance?

A lot of the confusion concerning salvation is caused by a misunderstanding of the role of repentance. Some subscribe to a *"quick prayerism"* mentality where you just get someone to pray a prayer without taking much time to really discuss what sin is or God's view on it, insisting that repentance has nothing to do with salvation. On the opposite extreme, many Christians try to get the lost person to "give up" all his sins and promise to stop doing them all before they'll lead him in the prayer of faith. Neither view is biblical, the truth is somewhere in the middle.

When considering the subject of repentance in relation to a lost man's salvation it is very important that one recognize the fact that the clearest verses in the Bible on salvation say little to nothing about repentance. It is important that we only emphasize something as much as God does. So while repentance plays a part, it needs to be put in its proper perspective.

Where is the repentance in these verses?

Romans 10:8-13, "But what saith it? The word is nigh thee, even in thy mouth, and in thy heart: that is, the word of faith, which we preach;

3

9) That if thou shalt confess with thy mouth the Lord Jesus, and shalt <u>believe in thine heart</u> that God hath raised him from the dead, thou shalt be saved.

10) For <u>with the heart man believeth unto righteousness</u>; and with the mouth confession is made unto salvation.

11) For the scripture saith, <u>Whosoever believeth on him shall not be ashamed.</u>

12) For there is no difference between the Jew and the Greek: for the same Lord over all is rich unto all that call upon him.

13) For <u>whosoever shall call upon the name of the Lord</u> shall be saved."

Gal 3:1-3, "O foolish Galatians, who hath bewitched you, that ye should not obey the truth, before whose eyes Jesus Christ hath been evidently set forth, crucified among you?

2) This only would I learn of you, Received ye the Spirit by the works of the law, or by the <u>hearing of faith?</u>

3) Are ye so foolish? <u>having begun in the Spirit, are ye now made perfect by the flesh?"</u>

Eph. 2:8-9, "<u>For by grace are ye saved through faith;</u> and that not of yourselves: it is the gift of God:

9) Not of works, lest any man should boast."

Romans 3:22, "Even <u>the righteousness of God which is by faith</u> of Jesus Christ unto all and upon all them that believe: for there is no difference:

28) Therefore we conclude that <u>a man is justified by faith</u> without the deeds of the law."

Romans 5:1-2, "<u>Therefore being justified by faith</u>, we have peace with God through our Lord Jesus Christ:"

2) By whom also <u>we have access by faith into this grace wherein we stand</u>, and rejoice in hope of the glory of God."

True story: a young Bible school student was leading another man to the Lord. This man knew he was a sinner and desperately wanted to be saved. He knew he was lost and was ready to pray and ask for salvation. The Christian was grilling the lost man, hoping to guarantee that he had "properly repented" before praying the prayer of faith. When all sins had been thoroughly examined and cast aside, the lost man's girlfriend pulled up in the driveway. *"Can you say no to her? Can you reject her?"* was the foolhardy question of the young student. The man, lost in his sins, said no.

Only God knows if he ever trusted Christ.

Must the man dying of thirst jump through a ring of fire, stand on his head, and crawl on crushed glass? Must he *earn his salvation* through repentance? Where is this taught in the Bible? Where in the Bible is the exact formula of salvation-granting repentance? Wouldn't it be hypocritical or inconsistent for a Christian who doesn't have everything straightened out in his life to insist that the lost man must repent of everything before *he* can pray the prayer of faith? Which sins must be repented of and which ones are okay to be left ignored? Where is this in the Bible, and how is this supposed to be "simple?"

Yes, repentance plays a part in salvation, in fact it goes hand in hand with faith, but all God expects of a lost man is to repent of *who he is and what he's trusting in.* A lost man must know he's a sinner and that he needs a Saviour – nothing more and nothing less. He must understand that Jesus Christ is the only way of salvation, and that he himself is a sinner deserving of Hell.

Repentance, when it comes to salvation, is not quitting every sin and then trusting Christ. First of all, that would be works, and secondly, a lost man *can't quit* his sin without having the new nature and the Holy Spirit in him to help him. Most Christians *today* fail to take hold of the power they have over sin in Christ, but must a lost man somehow do so *before salvation*?

I Cor. 2:14, "But the natural man receiveth not the things of the Spirit of God: for they are foolishness unto him: <u>neither can he know them, because they are spiritually discerned.</u>"

Eph. 2:1, "And you hath he quickened, <u>who were dead in trespasses and sins;</u>"

There are cases where repentance is preached along with salvation in the Bible. This doesn't mean that it was the repentance that saved them. As a preacher put it one time: repentance qualifies a man for salvation, but it's the faith that saves him. Understanding that you're not good enough or that your religion is not good enough is a painful process for most. That process still doesn't save a man, but it gets him to where he needs to be to trust Christ. When someone comes to the end of that process, they have reached a "place of repentance" and are ready to trust Christ. At that point, their hearts and minds have turned towards Christ. Quitting sin is what people do to become disciples, not what they do to get saved.

Having said all that, does that mean that repentance doesn't play a part in salvation? Of course not – but repentance doesn't save anyone any more than a fiery sermon in a tent meeting on a hot day in July does. A Holy Ghost-convicting song service doesn't save anyone, weeping tears of repentance doesn't save anyone, and having a glorious experience doesn't save anyone.

Gal. 3:11, "But that no man is justified by the law in the sight of God, it is evident: for, _The just shall live by faith._"

The reason this needs to be said is because when people doubt their salvation they usually always wind up asking these sort of questions:

1. Can I remember a specific day and time?
2. Did I repent correctly?
3. Did I listen to the right spirit?
4. Did I say the right words?
5. Did I really mean it?
6. Did I feel a difference?

"Did I..." Do you see where the emphasis is shifting when you start asking yourself those questions? It's going back on yourself and on an experience in the past that you probably don't even remember.

7

Preparation ≠ Salvation / Faith = Salvation

What does all this have to do with a person today doubting his or her salvation? When you start doubting whether or not you repented *correctly* or if you felt and said things the right way, even though you think you are wondering if you were saved correctly, what you are really wondering is whether or not you were *prepared* correctly.

You are saved by faith alone in Jesus Christ, how you were prepared doesn't matter anymore.

Anything else, be it repentance, preaching, feelings, the words spoken in prayer, the color of the carpet and the preaching behind the pulpit may all play a part in getting you to the point of where you need to be to believe – but they do not save you.

If right now you understand that without Christ you are a hopelessly lost sinner who can do nothing to save yourself, you believe that Christ died to pay the penalty **for** your sins and rose again, and you are trusting in Jesus Christ to save you - then you are saved, right now.

Drinking the water is what quenches the thirst; the color of the cup or how you get the cup doesn't matter.

Rev. 22:17, "And the Spirit and the bride say, Come. And let him that heareth say, Come. And let him that is athirst come. And <u>whosoever will, let him take the water of life freely.</u>"

Chapter Two

Step One: Renegotiate Your Contract of Grace with God.

"...this grace wherein we stand, and rejoice in hope..."

Romans 5:2

Buying a house for the first time is always quite an experience. You make an offer, they counter. You counter the counter. They agree. Then there's an inspection, and it turns out there are some things wrong with the house. Everyone backs up and reconsiders. You had your heart set on the home, but now you're scared to buy it unless the current owner agrees to fix the problems with the house. So tentatively you make another offer, hoping it doesn't kill the deal. The owner gets mad at you now, because they needed you to buy their home so they could buy a different home on a bridge loan. This, of course, pushes the closing date out until the repairs can be made – even *if* they agree to them. Many of us have been there before and understand the stress that can lead up to the closing date, and we also understand the relief that follows once both parties have signed. Once it's signed, there's no going back; it's settled.

There are basically two types of contracts: unilateral and bilateral. A bilateral contract is the most common, which is an agreement between two parties. As long as both parties fulfill their end of the agreement, the contract remains in place.

When you got saved you took part in a unilateral contract. This contract is completely one-sided; all you do is sign on the bottom line and all the responsibility involved in getting you to Heaven lies with God. That's what grace is all about.

The terms of the contract are as follows:

1. You agree that you are sinner unable of saving yourself (Rom. 3:23).
2. You believe that Christ died for your sins and rose again according to the Gospel (I Cor. 15:1-4).
3. By faith, the best way you know how, you put all your trust in what Jesus did for you on a personal level, asking forgiveness of your sins (Rom. 10:8-13).

Once you sign on the dotted line there is nothing left for you to do to uphold this contract; no works before, no works afterwards. All the responsibility for getting you to Heaven lies upon God from that moment forever.

Therefore to lose your salvation you'd have to change the manner in which you were saved to begin with. You'd have to renegotiate this contract of grace and go so far as to change these crucial words that Christ spoke on the cross:

"It is finished."

You see, to lose your salvation you'd have to completely change the actual foundation of what you're saved by. A person is saved by the grace of God which comes by faith in what Christ did on the cross. The Bible is abundantly clear that works have nothing to do with actually getting saved. Looking at things logically, if good works can't save a man then why would you think that bad works could reverse a person's salvation? Even in Paul's day this idea of being kept by works had begun to creep into the church of Galatia.

Gal. 3:1-7, 11, "O foolish Galatians, who hath bewitched you, that ye should not obey the truth, before whose eyes Jesus Christ hath been evidently set forth, crucified among you?

2) This only would I learn of you, Received ye the Spirit by the works of the law, or by the hearing of faith?

3) Are ye so foolish? having begun in the Spirit, are ye now made perfect by the flesh?

4) Have ye suffered so many things in vain? if it be yet in vain.

5) He therefore that ministereth to you the Spirit, and worketh miracles among you, doeth he it by the works of the law, or by the hearing of faith?

6) Even as Abraham believed God, and it was accounted to him for righteousness.

7) Know ye therefore that they which are of faith, the same are the children of Abraham.

11) But that <u>no man is justified by the law in the sight of God</u>, it is evident: for, <u>The just shall live by faith.</u>"

Paul asks the people in this church why they've been "bewitched" into thinking that after being saved by grace through faith that they somehow need to be continually justified in the eyes of God through works. We're not talking about people who were trying to decide whether or not Jesus was really the Christ or not – these folks were already saved Christians.

They already had the Holy Spirit, they had fruit, and God was working miracles amongst them. In spite of all that, they felt somehow they had to earn it; earn it *after* they were already saved. No genuinely saved person ever thinks they have to earn it before they're saved, or they wouldn't be saved! Somehow, someway, the same man-centered philosophy that crept into the Galatian church has crept into the hearts of many Christians today.

Eph. 2:8-9, "For <u>by grace are ye saved</u> through faith; and that not of yourselves: it is the gift of God: 9) <u>Not of works, lest any man should boast.</u>"

Romans 4:4, "<u>But to him that worketh not, but believeth</u> on him that justifieth the ungodly, his faith is counted for righteousness."

These verses are very familiar to the typical Christian. We use them for witnessing to others and showing them the free grace that is found in Jesus Christ. Never forget that verse nine states that if we could earn it, men would boast. No one is going to be boasting in Heaven about how they earned their spot there.

So why would anyone think that God views works any different *after* salvation? Why would God save you by free grace, and then reverse that free grace and make you have to *earn* it the rest of your life?

Romans 3:25-26, "Whom God hath set forth to be a <u>propitiation through faith</u> in his blood, to declare his righteousness for the remission of sins that are past, through the forbearance of God;
26) To declare, I say, at this time his righteousness: that he might be just, and <u>the justifier of him which believeth in Jesus.</u>"

Propitiation means "satisfaction."

The Bible says that when a man is lost that the *"wrath of God abideth on him"* (John 3:36). That wrath is satisfied only by the blood of Christ. The only way to have access to that blood is through faith.

This basic truth is the foundation of our salvation. It doesn't change after we are saved.

Chapter Three

Step Two: Change When You Get Eternal Life.

"He that believeth on the Son hath everlasting life..."

John 3:36

There is a terrible and devastating doctrine that has been taught by those who support works salvation; it's called *"the sin of presumption."* While there is a sin of presumption taught in the Bible, it's not what is taught by these Pharisees. This so-called sin is *presuming* to know for sure that if you were to die today you'd wind up in Heaven.

The primary characteristic of a Pharisee is that he puts heavy burdens on men that God never intended for them to have. God wants His children to live joyful lives, and while we're almost guaranteed to suffer persecution or be called to sacrifice for our Savior in one way or another, we can and should do it with peace, knowing that regardless of what happens here we have a home in Heaven.

I John 5:13, "These things have I written unto you that believe on the name of the Son of God; that ye may know that ye have eternal life, and that ye may believe on the name of the Son of God."

It's very clear in I John 5:13 that we can *know* we have eternal life.

Here's where the confusion lies with those who teach *"the sin of presumption":* they think you get eternal life later, not now.

The Bible teaches that everlasting life and eternal life are a present possession. It is not something that is promised to you later on, after you die. It's not something you can only hope to get or earn; it's something that you have in your possession *right away* from the moment you believe.

John 3:15-16, "That whosoever believeth in him should not perish, but <u>have eternal life.</u>
16) For God so loved the world, that he gave his only begotten Son, that whosoever believeth in him should not perish, but <u>have everlasting life."</u>

John 6:47, "Verily, verily, I say unto you, He that believeth on me <u>hath everlasting life."</u>

I John 5:11, "And this is the record, that <u>God hath given to us eternal life</u>, and this life is in his Son.
12) <u>He that hath the Son hath life; and he that hath not the Son of God hath not life."</u>

It doesn't get any simpler than that.

To take it further, and to better understand why it is you have eternal life immediately upon salvation, let's look at what happens when a baby takes its first breath.

While in the womb, the baby gets everything it needs to grow and develop just by being attached to its mother. Without eating it absorbs nutrition from its mother, and without breathing it has oxygen flowing through its blood. Once a baby takes its first breath, the dormant lungs are filled with air and the baby could never again go back into its mother's womb. It has received a life of its own, never to be the same again.

Upon trusting Christ, we have spiritually taken that first breath of everlasting life. He *is* that everlasting life that is given to us. When you get life, you get Jesus Christ, and unless He goes defunct, that everlasting life you receive will last forever; not because of who you are, but because of who Jesus is.

Col. 3:4, "When Christ, who is our life, shall appear, then shall ye also appear with him in glory."

John 6:33, "And Jesus said unto them, I am the bread of life: he that cometh to me shall never hunger; and he that believeth on me shall never thirst."

John 11:25, "Jesus said unto her, I am the resurrection, and the life: he that believeth in me, though he were dead, yet shall he live:"

John 14:6, "Jesus saith unto him, I am the way, the truth, and the life: no man cometh unto the Father, but by me."

Malachi 3:6, "<u>For I am the LORD, I change not;</u> therefore ye sons of Jacob are not consumed."

Chapter Four

Step Three: Overpower God.

"Being confident of this very thing, that he which hath begun a good work in you will perform it until the day of Jesus Christ:"

Philippians 1:6

As we go along, it should become more and more apparent to the child of God that just as salvation is all about God, so too is staying saved.

The Angel of the Lord wrestled with Jacob all night long. Jacob wouldn't let go unless He gave him a blessing. At the breaking of the day, the Angel insisted that Jacob let go; when Jacob wouldn't all He had to do was simply touch his thigh – and Jacob walked with a limp the rest of his life.

Is there anything more powerful than God? How does one even express or try to explain the power of God? We can look at the forces of nature: hurricanes, tsunamis, earthquakes, and volcanoes, but even all these things are just a glimpse at the awesome power of God.

Is. 45:6, "That they may know from the rising of the sun, and from the west, that there is none beside me. I am the LORD, and there is none else."

The reason it is important to reflect on the magnitude of God's power is because it is *that* power that holds you and keeps you after you are saved.

We are all geared towards earning what we have. Good parents teach their children that they must earn a living; that if you don't work, you don't eat (II Thess. 3:10). We work hard our whole lives to earn our way in this world, and there's nothing wrong with that.

When it comes to our salvation, however, there is nothing we can do to earn it. As the bumper sticker says, *"If you could earn it, why did He die?"*

We look in awe at the energy created during the industrial age and into the information age. From nuclear fusion to the atom bomb to a cell phone more powerful than the "supercomputers" that used to fill entire rooms. All this power and energy made by man is a drop in the bucket compared to the power of God.

Is. 40:15, "Behold, the nations are as a drop of a bucket, and are counted as the small dust of the balance: behold, he taketh up the isles as a very little thing."

The power behind our salvation is God Himself. After trusting Christ, the guarantee of our eternal destiny lies within God's hands, not our own. We are kept by the power of God!

I Peter 1:5, "<u>Who are kept by the power of God</u> through faith unto salvation ready to be revealed in the last time."

So to lose your salvation you'd have to be able to overpower God in one way or another.

I Cor. 1:7-9, "So that ye come behind in no gift; waiting for the coming of our Lord Jesus Christ:
8) <u>Who shall also confirm you unto the end</u>, that ye may be blameless in the day of our Lord Jesus Christ.
9) <u>God is faithful</u>, by whom ye were called unto the fellowship of his Son Jesus Christ our Lord."

We see here that it is God that confirms us unto the end. He is our foundation, our Rock, our hope, everything we'll ever need from time until eternity.

John 10:27-30, "My sheep hear my voice, and I know them, and they follow me:
28) And I give unto them eternal life; and <u>they shall never perish</u>, <u>neither shall any man pluck them out of my hand.</u>
29) My Father, which gave them me, <u>is greater than all</u>; and <u>no man</u> is able to pluck them out of my Father's hand.
30) <u>I and my Father are one.</u>"

There are so many wonderful things in that passage! Simply put, in verse 28 Jesus says, *"They shall never perish."* There is no exception put forth. There is no loophole, exemption, or exclusion given. Once you get saved, you have everlasting life as a present possession and you are guaranteed to never perish, no matter what.

To back this statement up even further, Christ demonstrates what Peter said by telling the people that God the Father is greater than all and no man is able to pluck anyone out of His hand. A child of God is safe and secure forever within the mighty hands of God the Father and Jesus Christ, and no man is powerful enough to change that.

Jude 24-25, "Now unto <u>him that is able to keep you from falling, and to present you faultless</u> before the presence of his glory with exceeding joy,
25 To the only wise God our Saviour, be glory and majesty, dominion and power, both now and ever. Amen."

He is able, and He has *promised* to deliver.

Chapter Five

Step Four: Make a Liar out of God.

"And whosoever liveth and believeth in me shall never die. Believest thou this?"

John 11:26

David said all men are liars (Ps. 116:11) and Jesus said that He knew what was within man (John 2:25). David lied, Abraham lied, Paul lied, and Peter lied, but they're all in Heaven today.

When remembering the falsely labeled "sin of presumption," let's not forget that not only are these liars *in Heaven* but that they all had *assurance* of the fact that they'd wind up in eternity with God after death. David spoke about knowing one day he would go to his son (II Sam. 12:23). Jesus said that Abraham rejoiced to see His day (John 8:56). Paul had assurance of his salvation (II Tim. 1:12, Phil. 1:6) and so did Peter (I Peter 1:3-4). Apparently the "sin of presumption" wasn't enough to knock *them* out.

It's obvious the reason these men went to Heaven wasn't because they weren't liars (because they were); it was because *God* isn't a liar. When He gave David the *"sure mercies of David,"* God wasn't about to go back on

His promise just because David did a few minor things like lying, murdering, and committing adultery.

Look at these following verses concerning your salvation and pay close attention to the deliberate and unconditional promises:

John 5:24, "Verily, verily, I say unto you, He that heareth my word, and believeth on him that sent me, hath everlasting life, and shall not come into condemnation; but is passed from death unto life."

John 6:37, "All that the Father giveth me shall come to me; and him that cometh to me I will in no wise cast out."

Matthew 28:20, "Teaching them to observe all things whatsoever I have commanded you: and, lo, I am with you alway, even unto the end of the world. Amen."

These verses are as clear as it can get. Jesus doesn't list out any special sin that will cause a person to *"lose it."* The promise is put out there repeatedly that if you believe you will never come into condemnation, and that under no circumstances would someone be *"cast out."*

In order to lose your salvation, you'd have to make a liar out of God. This is the same God who promised the entire nation of Israel that one day they'd leave Egypt (Ex. 3:7-8), promised to them when the Messiah would come the first time (Dan. 9:24-26), and told them that after being scattered they would one day return to their

23

homeland (Jer. 30:3, partially fulfilled in 1948). God promised Paul on a prisoner boat that no one would die while going through a storm (Acts 27:23-24), and He kept His word.

Think about it: God promised a couple of old people in the desert that they'd have children and of those children would come a great nation. To top it off, they laughed at God when He made that promise – but He still kept His word.

He has a great track record of keeping His promises.

Do you really think you're going to be the person, who as you're thrown into Hell says *"But God, you said 'him that cometh to me I will in no wise cast out....'"*

God keeps His promises, for you to lose your salvation and go to Hell you'd have to get God to do something He is incapable of: lying.

Titus 1:2, "In hope of eternal life, which God, that cannot lie, promised before the world began;"

Chapter Six

Step Five: Separate Yourself from God's Love.

"...Yea, I have loved thee with an everlasting love..."

Jeremiah 31:3

The song goes, *"Could we with ink the ocean fill, and were the skies of parchment made, were every stalk on Earth a quill, and every man a scribe by trade; to write the love of God above would drain the ocean dry, nor could the scroll contain the whole, though stretched from sky to sky."*

Like so many things in the Bible there really isn't any way to completely understand the love of God; the best you can do is to simply believe what God said. God said He loves the child of God with an everlasting love that will never end.

Eph. 3:17-19, "That Christ may dwell in your hearts by faith; that ye, being rooted and grounded in love,

18) May be able to comprehend with all saints what is the breadth, and length, and depth, and height;

19) And to know the <u>love of Christ, which passeth knowledge</u>, that ye might be filled with all the fulness of God."

God loves the Christian so much that He has explicitly promised to never leave or forsake him. How many marriages in our day and age have begun with a promise and ended with heartache? Are we to believe that God is going to err in the same ways that humans do? At the root of the idea that a Christian can lose his salvation is the thought that what God does for you isn't enough and ultimately God *Himself* isn't enough for you!

Romans 8:38-39, "For I am persuaded, that neither death, nor life, nor angels, nor principalities, nor powers, nor things present, <u>nor things to come</u>,
39) Nor height, nor depth, nor any other creature, <u>shall be able to separate us from the love of God</u>, which is in Christ Jesus our Lord."

This is undoubtedly the greatest single passage on the doctrine of eternal security in the Bible. It shows that under no circumstance can a Christian in this age lose his salvation.

Even though the plain truth of this passage clearly shows the eternal relationship of love that a child of God has, many times when presented with this verse the contrarian will claim, *"But you can separate yourself!"* This is ridiculous and grasping at straws. If you could separate yourself from the love of God, you would be separated from God by something that happened *after you were saved.* In other words, you got saved, and then lost it. The verse clearly shows that this isn't possible because *"nor things to come"* means that nothing that could ever happen in the future would ever separate you from God's love.

God's love is in Jesus Christ. God is love; outside of God there is no love.

I John 4:14, "And we have known and believed the love that God hath to us. God is love; and he that dwelleth in love dwelleth in God, and God in him."

God doesn't love a lost person the same way He loves a child of God. God so loved the world that He sent His Son – God offers His love to a lost man to receive, but the further a man gets away from God's Son, the further he gets away from God's love. Some have made the argument that God doesn't love a lost man at all. That is not clearly taught in the Scriptures, but what is clear is that a lost man lives his life in constant sin, enmity with God, and under the wrath of God:

Prov. 21:4, "An high look, and a proud heart, and the plowing of the wicked, is sin."

Rom. 8:7, "Because the carnal mind is enmity against God: for it is not subject to the law of God, neither indeed can be."

Rom. 5:10, "For if, when we were enemies, we were reconciled to God by the death of his Son, much more, being reconciled, we shall be saved by his life."

John 3:36, "He that believeth on the Son hath everlasting life: and he that believeth not the Son shall not see life; but the <u>wrath of God abideth on him.</u>"

When that lost man dies without Christ he has exhausted any hope to know real love. The scorner has asked repeatedly, *"How could a loving God send anyone to Hell?"* Ironically, there is some truth to the point the person is trying to make because God doesn't send anyone that He loves to Hell. Does "love win?" Yes, but love is only found in Jesus Christ, and if you're not in Him you won't "win." If a man goes to Hell, that guarantees that he's managed to avoid God's offer of love for the last time and there *is no love left for him*.

That can't happen to a Christian. Nothing that could ever come in the future could ever separate a Christian from the love of God. To those who trust in good works but never accept Christ, He will say that He never knew them to begin with - *not* that He knew them, they blew it, and then He forgot them.

Matt. 7:22-23, "Many will say to me in that day, Lord, Lord, have we not prophesied in thy name? and in thy name have cast out devils? and in thy name done many wonderful works?
23) And then will I profess unto them, <u>I never knew you: depart from me</u>, ye that work iniquity."

God is not like man. God is faithful and keeps His promises. He is enough, He is all you will ever need and more than you could ever hope to have.

Heb. 13:5, "Let your conversation be without covetousness; and be content with such things as ye have: for he hath said, I will never leave thee, nor forsake thee."

Chapter Seven

Step Six: Fire Your Representative.

"...the author and finisher of our faith..."

Hebrews 12:2

A black and bony finger points down through the heavens as the wicked one screams to God the Father, *"You see what he just did? You call that a son of God? Surely you can't be serious! After what he just did to You?"*

Sitting next to the Father, the Son lifts His scarred hands and says, *"The price has been paid. I'm his advocate; I'm his representative and high priest... I'm his sacrifice. The price has been paid."*

In declaring to be the author and finisher of our faith Jesus Christ has accepted all the responsibility *and glory* for getting us to Heaven. Any other way would mean that we were the finishers of our faith.

Before Christ, it wasn't all that uncommon for a person, group, or nation to go to a prophet or a man of God and ask him to intercede for them. Under the law, sinners absolutely needed priests to help them offer sacrifices for their sins. In other words, before Christ you *had* middlemen between God and other men. That ended at Calvary though, and *now* Jesus Christ is our representative.

I Tim. 2:5-6, "For there is one God, and <u>one mediator between God and men</u>, the man Christ Jesus;
6) Who gave himself a ransom for all, to be testified in due time."

There is one mediator, Jesus Christ, who stands between us and God. There are no mediatrixes or strange men dressed in black with funny looking collars ordained by God in the New Testament. If the Jewish priests of the Old Testament *who God used mightily* are no good today, then certainly *no man today* can represent you to God when it comes to the penalty of your sins and where you will spend eternity.

Hebrews 10:10-12, "By the which will we are sanctified through the offering of the body of Jesus Christ once for all.
11) And every priest standeth daily ministering and offering oftentimes the same sacrifices, which can never take away sins:
12) <u>But this man</u>, after he had offered one sacrifice for sins for ever, <u>sat down on the right hand of God;</u>"

Christ's sacrifice, once applied, sanctifies a person *"once for all."* Once again, no exclusions or exceptions are given. After offering this sacrifice, it says that Jesus Christ sat down at the right hand of the throne of God.

From up in Heaven, He is our representative; He is our advocate.

I John 2:1, "My little children, these things write I unto you, that ye sin not. And if any man sin, <u>we have an advocate with the Father, Jesus Christ the righteous:</u>"

Rom. 8:34, "Who is he that condemneth? It is Christ that died, yea rather, that is risen again, who is even at the right hand of God, <u>who also maketh intercession for us.</u>"

Your lawyer, if you want to call Him that, is Jesus Christ Himself. He is our advocate with the Father and our representative. Should the accuser of the brethren (Rev. 12:10) ever bring charges to God the Father against us, our defense attorney is Jesus Christ. Our advocate brings the same argument to our defense every time: *the penalty has already been paid.*

Now going back to our scene in Heaven, how ridiculous would it be if after Christ stood up to defend you, you somehow found a way to interrupt the conversation. "No, that's okay, I'm okay, I can represent myself... I've got it handled, I've got this!"

Such an idea is preposterous! Jesus is your High Priest standing between you and *a guilty ruling* in God's courtroom. Christ is your middleman and representative – He's the reason you're not going to Hell.

If you were to lose your salvation, you'd have to *fire* Him.

Chapter Eight

Step Seven: Commit Spiritual Identity Theft.

"...Abraham believed God, and it was counted unto him for righteousness."

Romans 4:3

So far in this study we've looked extensively at the promises of eternal life from several different angles, and while that's still going to be referenced, *from this point* on we're going to be looking more at some of the actual changes that happen to a Christian at the moment of salvation.

We are more than just forgiven when we ask for forgiveness that first time in prayer. According to the word of God there are some other really amazing things that happen to us.

When a person accepts Christ, *he* gets Christ's righteousness. The old dirty coat of sin is discarded as a robe of righteousness is placed on the believer. To lose your salvation somehow you'd have to either reverse the imputation of Christ's righteousness or dirty it up somehow.

In a beautiful picture of grace, Paul told Philemon that if his servant Onesimus had **"...wronged thee, or oweth thee ought, put that on mine account."** This is what Christ did for us on Calvary on an *eternal level.*

Think of two checking accounts - only the currency that gets deposited into these accounts is sin and righteousness. One account, before Salvation, has your name on it. Every day more and more sin is deposited into this account. The other account is Christ's, and every day it is filled with the currency of righteousness.

When you get saved, the names on the accounts switch – but the deposits are the same every day.

It's called imputation: to credit to the account of. In this illustration, the depositing that occurs is imputation. Every day your sins are no longer imputed to your account but Christ's righteousness *is,* and at the same time your sins are imputed to Christ's account on a *continual basis* – but they've been paid for forever.

Romans 4:6-8, "Even as David also describeth the blessedness of the man, unto <u>whom God imputeth righteousness without works,</u>
7) Saying, Blessed are they whose iniquities are forgiven, and whose sins are covered.
8) Blessed is the man to whom <u>the Lord will not impute sin.</u>"

In this passage we see two things going on. First of all, God is imputing righteousness to the believer without him doing anything to earn it, and secondly, the Lord is *not* imputing the sin of the believer to his account.

We're all going to keep sinning when we get saved, but what we learn from this passage is that although we sin God does *not* hold it against us in the next life.

Rom. 4:3, 22-24, "For what saith the scripture? Abraham believed God, and it was counted unto him for righteousness.

22) And therefore <u>it was imputed to him for righteousness.</u>

23) Now it was <u>not written for his sake alone, that it was imputed to him;</u>

24) <u>But for us also, to whom it shall be imputed, if we believe on him</u> that raised up Jesus our Lord from the dead;"

II Cor. 5:19, 21, "To wit, that God was in Christ, reconciling the world unto himself, <u>not imputing their trespasses unto them;</u> and hath committed unto us the word of reconciliation.

21) For he hath made him to be sin for us, who knew no sin; that <u>we might be made the righteousness of God in him.</u>"

We get Christ's righteousness, and on Calvary He took on our sin.

At this point questions may arise about sins in this life and whether or not they have bearing on a Christian's life today. Yes, of course they do. This has to do with the *standing* of a Christian versus the *state* of a Christian.

Your *standing* is that you are a child of God and nothing can change that. Your eternal relationship with God is based entirely upon whether or not you've trusted Christ.

Your *state* is determined upon your relationship with God at any given moment. A child can rebel against his father, but it doesn't change who that son is and who that father is. They are both related to each other and whether they like it or not they still have each other's blood in their veins.

So, in order to undo this kind of bank account setup that God has established, someone would have to hijack Christ's bank account and sell it on the spiritual black market, where another person could impute sins to Christ's account to wreck the salvation of millions of people. Someone would have to commit spiritual identity theft.

How *bizarre* and preposterous! So too is the idea that you can lose what God gave you in the gift of salvation.

No matter what you do, your sin will *not* be credited to your account in the afterlife. It is abundantly clear that your sins are no longer imputed to you and that from the moment of salvation it is Christ's righteousness that is. For those who struggle with the mistakes of the past and the temptations of today, please understand that your sin is no longer imputed to you eternally. While you may deal with the consequences *in this life,* God has *mercifully* forgiven you to where in eternity you do not have to pay the penalty for your sin.

Chapter Nine

Step Eight: Revoke the Cosmic Law of Double Jeopardy.

"For the truth's sake, which dwelleth in us, and shall be with us for ever."

II John 1:2

There's nothing more troublesome in a marriage or any relationship than when someone feels the need to pull things out of the past and reexamine it again. This is the cause for so many broken vases, planters, and other shattered objects that can be tossed during lively discussions of marital bliss. Hopefully not in your home, but you get the idea: nothing's more frustrating than having to deal with something that you've felt was already taken care of a long time ago. *It's like being convicted of the same crime twice.*

The legal term of double-jeopardy refers basically to the idea of being tried a second time for the same offense after you've been found innocent. If you've been found guilty in some cases it is possible to appeal, but if you're found innocent you can not be tried again for that crime.

Thus enters the doctrine of justification: a judicial act to declare one to be innocent.

Upon salvation, God judicially declares the sinner to be just, perfecting him forever.

Heb. 10:12,14, "But this man, after he had offered one sacrifice for sins for ever, sat down on the right hand of God;
14) For by one offering he hath perfected for ever them that are sanctified."

This verse can be applied to several aspects of eternal security, but in this case the focus is on the fact that a Christian is "perfected for ever." However, if you know anything about Christians, you should know that they can be *real stinkers.* The idea of being justified doesn't change who the Christian is in the sense that it *doesn't* actually do anything to him. He isn't made righteous, he doesn't have his sins rerouted away from him (as in the case where God doesn't impute his sin to him), and he isn't made a new creature by justification. All those things happen to a Christian at the moment of salvation – but those things have nothing to do with justification.

Justification doesn't change your character; it changes your *standing* with God. All justification is about is God saying something is so. This is the same God that spoke the world into existence, spoke Lazarus out of the tomb, and knocked over a group of rabble-rousers by simply saying, *"I am He."* When God says something, it is so.

God *declares* a sinner to be just based upon one qualification only:

Rom. 4:1-5, "What shall we say then that Abraham our father, as pertaining to the flesh, hath found?

2) For <u>if Abraham were justified by works, he hath whereof to glory; but not before God</u>.

3) For what saith the scripture? <u>Abraham believed God</u>, and it was counted unto him for righteousness.

4) Now to him that worketh is the reward not reckoned of grace, but of debt.

5) But to him that worketh not, but believeth on him that justifieth the ungodly, his <u>faith is counted for righteousness</u>."

The only thing that is going to cause the Judge of All the Earth to declare you to be just is faith. Works do not justify a man before God. Pay special attention to the tail end of verse two where it says, ***"...but not before God."*** It's talking about the "what if" of works. Do works justify? What that verse is telling you is that if works *do* justify, they don't justify *"before God."* The Holy Spirit was very wise in putting in this passage because of the corresponding passage in James 2.

James 2:21-24, "Was <u>not Abraham our father justified by works</u>, when he had offered Isaac his son upon the altar?

22) Seest thou how faith wrought with his works, and by works was faith made perfect?

23) And the scripture was fulfilled which saith, <u>Abraham believed God, and it was imputed unto him for righteousness:</u> and he was called the Friend of God.

24) Ye see then how that <u>by works a man is justified, and not by faith only</u>."

Anyone with any door-to-door visitation experience will have this passage pulled on them. Usually it's just a loose quotation without the Bible actually being opened, but regardless it is pulled on Bible believers *all the time.*

James 2 can not be understood without Romans 4 to explain it. Romans 4:2 clearly demonstrates that man *can not* be justified in the eyes of God by works, and that Abraham *was not* justified by works in any way before God.

That doesn't mean we should throw James 2 out; it has a very valuable teaching involved. Remember, justification is a *judicial act.* It doesn't change whether or not a person is *guilty in the sense that he did the crime or not.* All it does is *declare* the person to be just; it doesn't actually make him just. He has been acquitted. There is absolutely no contradiction between James 2 and Romans 4 when you read it understanding the *correct* definition of justification.

By faith we are declared to be just before God, but in the eyes of man talk is cheap if there isn't anything to back it up in the life of the believer. The justification in James 2 is the idea of being declared just in the *eyes of man* – not in the eyes of God.

James 2:18, 20 "Yea, <u>a man may say</u>, Thou hast faith, and I have works: shew me thy faith without thy works, and <u>I will shew thee my faith by my works.</u>
20) But <u>wilt thou know, O vain man</u>, that faith without works is dead?"

RICK SCHWORER

This entire controversial passage has nothing to do with God knowing the man is just or not. God has already tried the man, pardoned him, declared him just, and perfected him forever. This has to do with what man sees. **"But wilt thou know, O vain man..."** not "will God know..." God already knows! Verse 18 says that a man will show his faith *by his works*. Why would God need further evidence of your faith once you've already been justified in His courtroom? Your friends, neighbors, and coworkers need to see your works or they are not going to believe you have real faith.

Rom. 4:2, "For if Abraham were justified by works, he hath whereof to glory; but not before God."

Rom. 3:26, "To declare, I say, at this time his righteousness: that he might be just, and the justifier of him which believeth in Jesus."

They say that lightning never strikes the same place twice. When the gavel comes down and words, "Pardoned, not guilty, the price has been paid," are spoken, you are forever made perfect in the eyes of God.

This may not make sense to the average person, but it doesn't have to. How many times have you seen a man who from all appearances seems be declared "innocent" in reality be guilty *(does a white SUV fleeing from the cops back in the '90s ring a bell?)*? Does being declared innocent actually make him innocent? Yes and no. Being declared innocent doesn't change whether or not he committed the crime; it only declares him to be *innocent of the consequences.* You see a man can be guilty as sin, but be fortunate enough *to get off the hook.* That's what happens to a sinner when he gets saved, even though he did the crime, he is forever declared to be just by God. It doesn't change who he is or what he did; it's simply a judicial declaration that can never be overturned.

There is no further trial or opportunity for a case to be made against a Christian, he is declared innocent in the eyes of God for all time and eternity. You'd have to rewrite the laws in Heaven to undo this.

Chapter Ten

Step Nine: Disinherit Christ from What God Promised Him.

"The Spirit itself beareth witness with our spirit, that we are the children of God:"

Romans 8:16

In trying to comfort the persecuted saints, Peter reminds them that they are kept by the power of God and they have an eternal inheritance waiting for them. This inheritance is two-fold. First of all, it's the mansion that Jesus Christ went to prepare for us in Heaven, and secondly, it is the new body that a Christian receives at the resurrection.

I Peter 1:3-5, "Blessed be the God and Father of our Lord Jesus Christ, which according to his abundant mercy hath begotten us again unto a lively hope by the resurrection of Jesus Christ from the dead,
4) To an <u>inheritance incorruptible, and undefiled, and that fadeth not away, reserved in heaven for you,</u>
5) Who are kept by the power of God through faith unto salvation ready to be revealed in the last time."

John 14:2, "In my Father's house are <u>many mansions:</u> if it were not so, I would have told you. I go to prepare a place for you."

I Cor. 15:52, In a moment, in the twinkling of an eye, at the last trump: for the trumpet shall sound, and <u>the dead shall be raised incorruptible, and we shall be changed.</u>"

This is an inheritance that is promised to the Christian by God the Father. You get it because you are one of God's children and a brother to Christ. Jesus Christ is God in the flesh, the second member of the Trinity (or Godhead), and the only begotten Son of God the Father. Jesus was begotten in time, not in eternity. He is as much God as God the Father is, it's just that His human body was prepared for Him at a specific time.

Heb. 10:5, "<u>Wherefore when he cometh into the world</u>, he saith, Sacrifice and offering thou wouldest not, but a <u>body hast thou prepared me:</u>"

Ps. 2:7, "I will declare the decree: the LORD hath said unto me, Thou art my Son; <u>this day have I begotten thee.</u>"

Take special note of the fact that Christ was begotten on a specific day. The first day was during creation, so He was begotten sometime after creation. Clearly the day in which Christ took upon Himself human form was the day in which He was begotten. Jesus is God's only begotten Son and will forever be the only begotten of the

Father, but He is *also* the firstborn of many brethren according to the Bible.

In plainer words, Jesus isn't just your Saviour and Advocate, but He's also your brother.

Rom. 8:29, "For whom he did foreknow, he also did predestinate to be conformed to the image of his Son, <u>that he might be the firstborn among many brethren.</u>"

I John 3:2, "Beloved, now are we the sons of God, and <u>it doth not yet appear what we shall be:</u> but we know that, when he shall appear, <u>we shall be like him;</u> for we shall see him as he is."

Somehow our resurrection bodies are going to be very much like Christ's own resurrection body. It says we will be conformed to "His image." It also states that it's not clear in the Bible exactly what we're going to be, but that our bodies are going to be something "like Him."

Not only are we promised an inheritance, but so is Christ:

Ps. 2:6-9, "Yet have I set my king <u>upon my holy hill of Zion.</u>
7) I will declare the decree: the LORD hath said unto me, <u>Thou art my Son; this day have I begotten thee.</u>
8) Ask of me, and I <u>shall give thee the heathen for thine inheritance, and the uttermost parts of the earth for thy possession.</u>

9) Thou shalt break them with a <u>rod of iron;</u> thou shalt dash them in pieces like a potter's vessel."

Eph. 1:18, "The eyes of your understanding being enlightened; that ye may know what is the hope of his calling, and what the riches of the glory of <u>his inheritance in the saints,</u>"

We see Christ as receiving three things here for His inheritance:

1. The heathen. This is a reference to people in the Millennium. They are ruled with a rod of iron according to Revelation 12.

2. The uttermost parts of the Earth. This is speaking of the Earth itself during the Millennium when Christ rules from Jerusalem after the Second Coming. Take note of verse six that speaks of the king upon the holy hill of Zion.

3. The saints. Lastly, Christ's inheritance is the saints themselves.

Now imagine there being a legal document in Heaven, something like a will, that designated two legal entities to receive an inheritance upon a certain event or certain events. This inheritance is divided up between the two entities. Christ's inheritance is the first three we just looked at. The last three are our inheritance:

1. A new body.
2. A home in Heaven.
3. Christ. Not only does He get us, but we get Him as an inheritance.

This legal document has an inheritance of at least six items listed, if not more, to be distributed to Jesus Christ and to His fellow brethren. The next passage demonstrates not only one of the most amazing principles of the eternal security doctrine, but it also shows God's completely *breathtaking* grace like few others:

Rom. 8:16-17, "The Spirit itself beareth witness with our spirit, that we are the children of God:
17) And if children, then heirs; heirs of God, and joint-heirs with Christ; if so be that we suffer with him, that we may be also glorified together."

Galatians 4:7, "Wherefore thou art no more a servant, but a son; and if a son, then an heir of God through Christ."

Because we have been made God's children, we are heirs of God. Because of the fact that Christ also has an inheritance we are not limited to being heirs, but we are declared to be *"joint-heirs with Christ."* That means our name is on that legal document *with* Christ, and our future inheritance is tied together. If we do not receive our promised inheritance, then the document is nullified and neither does Christ.

For a born-again child of God to lose his salvation God the Father would not only have to break His promise of an inheritance to us, but He'd have to break His promise to His only begotten Son as well.

Chapter Eleven

Step Ten: Divorce Yourself from the Family of God.

"And he said, Abba, Father, all things are possible unto thee; take away this cup from me..."

"...whereby we cry, Abba, Father."

Mark 14:36, Romans 8:15

There is a difference between a child and a son. Prophesying of Christ, Isaiah said *"For unto us a child is born, unto us a son is given..."* (Is. 9:6). Take note that a child is born, but a son is something different. Christ as a child is a reference to His humanity, but as a son refers to His position within the Godhead.

There is a similarity with us. Being children of God, born into the family of God, we have a relationship with Christ. Being sons of God is very different, however. A child is just a child, but legally a son is an heir.

In Bible times the time of adoption would mean two basic things:

1) Just as it is today, adoption meant taking someone who was originally outside of your family and making him part of your family. It would be no different than a family

adopting an orphan or foster child today. That adopted child legally became a member of the new family. Adopted children today actually have just as strong a claim to inheritance as natural born children of the same family.

2) The other case meant a family taking its own naturally born child and adopting him. This adoption meant legally declaring the child a son and an heir. Before then the child had no bearing upon any possible inheritance. The relationship of the child with his parents never changed, but the position changed dramatically after being adopted by his own natural parents.

As Christians we are born into the family of God by the new birth, and then we are adopted and given the position of a son and a joint-heir with Christ.

Rom. 8:15, "For ye have not received the spirit of bondage again to fear; but <u>ye have received the Spirit of adoption</u>, whereby we cry, Abba, Father."

"Abba" is the Hebrew word for father. The reason it's in your English Bible is because God wanted you to see the distinction of spiritually coming from a Gentile family (before salvation) to a Jewish family (after salvation). You are now spiritually a Jew (Rom. 2:29) and are part of a brand new family – the family of God.

You have been *born* into this family as a *child* so that you may have a personal relationship with God the Father...

I Peter 1:23, "<u>Being born again</u>, not of corruptible seed, but <u>of incorruptible</u>, by the word of God, which liveth and abideth for ever."

...and have also been *adopted* into this family that you may have a position of an *heir* of the inheritance.

Gal. 4:5-7, "To redeem them that were under the law, that <u>we might receive the adoption of sons.</u>
6) And <u>because ye are sons</u>, God hath sent forth the Spirit of his Son into your hearts, crying, Abba, Father.
7) Wherefore thou <u>art no more a servant, but a son; and if a son, then an heir of God</u> through Christ."

This is a reference to the adoption of your spirit and soul; however there is still a *future* adoption of your body to come that will be discussed in the next chapter. Regardless, you are a son of God and for you to lose your salvation you'd have to figure out a way to legally divorce yourself from the family of God.

Chapter Twelve

Step Eleven: Unpredestinate Your Body.

"...I pray God your whole spirit and soul and body..."

I Thessalonians 5:23

There are three parts to a man: his spirit, soul, and body. The body is easy to understand, it's what's on the outside. In an upcoming chapter we'll look more closely at the spirit and soul, but this chapter deals with what is to become of our bodies and how that ties into having assurance of salvation.

There's an event coming and it's one of the most important events that will ever occur in human history. In fact you might be able to make the case that it is the most important event. It's the Second Coming of Jesus Christ. In Acts 1:11, as the disciples stood watching Jesus ascend into Heaven, two angels appeared and told them that one day Christ would return the same way He left: bodily.

Before Jesus Christ returns bodily to this Earth, the rapture of the church will occur at least seven years before. During this rapture the entire Earth will be interrupted in whatever it is that will be going on from town to town and city to city and millions of people will be taken from this Earth to Heaven. Shortly before that, the graves will be emptied and the bodies of the saints will be resurrected and caught up to Heaven as well.

Whether it's dead bodies being resurrected or alive bodies being taken to Heaven, every Christian's body at the Rapture of the church will be changed into a different kind of body. It's commonly called a glorified body. This body will never get sick again, feel pain, and best of all it won't have a sin nature anymore.

We are promised all of this and it is meant to be a comfort to the believer:

I Thess. 4:15-18, "For this we say unto you by the word of the Lord, that we which are alive and remain unto the coming of the Lord shall not prevent them which are asleep.

16) For the Lord himself shall descend from heaven with a shout, with the voice of the archangel, and with the trump of God: and <u>the dead in Christ shall rise first:</u>

17) Then we <u>which are alive and remain shall be caught up together with them</u> in the clouds, to meet the Lord in the air: and so shall we ever be with the Lord.

18) Wherefore comfort one another with these words."

I Cor. 15:52-55, "In a moment, in the twinkling of an eye, at the last trump: for the trumpet shall sound, and <u>the dead shall be raised incorruptible, and we shall be changed.</u>

53

53) For this <u>corruptible must put on incorruption,</u> and <u>this mortal must put on immortality.</u>

54) So when this corruptible shall have put on incorruption, and this mortal shall have put on immortality, then shall be brought to pass the saying that is written, Death is swallowed up in victory.

55) O death, where is thy sting? O grave, where is thy victory?"

This ties into eternal security in that we are not merely promised this (though that would certainly be enough), but God says we are predestinated to this.

Calvinists teach that certain people are predestinated to get saved. Nothing could be further from the truth; to teach such a thing would mean that God has also predestinated some to go to Hell. The Bible tells us that God doesn't want *anyone* to go to Hell.

II Peter 3:9, "The Lord is not slack concerning his promise, as some men count slackness; but is longsuffering to us-ward, <u>not willing that any should perish, but that all should come to repentance.</u>"

Calvinists who speak so much about eternal decrees, the "sovereign" grace of God, and the will of God completely ignore the fact that it is a *violation of God's will* every time someone rejects the gospel and goes to Hell.

Yes, we are predestinated to go to Heaven, but no one is predestinated to that until *after* he is saved.

Eph. 1:5, "Having <u>predestinated us unto the adoption of children</u> by Jesus Christ to himself, according to the good pleasure of his will,"

Rom. 8:23, "And not only they, but ourselves also, which have the firstfruits of the Spirit, even we ourselves groan within ourselves, <u>waiting for the adoption, to wit, the redemption of our body.</u>"

The words, "to wit," mean basically "to clarify." While our spirits and souls have been saved, cleaned, and even adopted – our bodies are just as rotten as ever before. We still have the same tendency to sin as we've always had. We're predestinated *to the adoption* and Paul clarifies that by telling us that the future adoption is the redemption of our bodies. This election and predestination comes by way of salvation – not before salvation:

I Peter 1:2, "Elect according to the foreknowledge of God the Father, <u>through sanctification of the Spirit, unto obedience and sprinkling of the blood of Jesus Christ:</u> Grace unto you, and peace, be multiplied."

The catalyst by which someone becomes part of the elect and is *predestinated* to get a new body is by the blood being applied and the spirit indwelling the man. That happens when a believer puts his faith in Christ at the moment of salvation, not before.

No one is ever predestinated to get saved – people are predestinated *after they are saved* and what they are predestinated to are things that have to do with receiving a new body or an eternal inheritance.

We'll read later on about the body of Christ. It is a spiritual organism and a reference to Christians after the cross and before the Rapture. Whenever the Bible talks about being "in Christ," it's talking about this group of people. The Bible talks about us being elect "in Christ" or elect "in Christ before the world began." That doesn't mean that Fred, Jim, and Larry were predestinated to get saved, it means that whoever is in the body of Christ is predestinated to get something after they are saved. It's predestination based upon *being in a group,* it's not individual election – *it's corporate election.* Meaning, basically, if you get "in Christ" then you are predestinated to get a new body one day and if you don't get "in Christ" then you are not. It's like saying "whoever gets *in the plane* is predestinated to land in Chicago." No one is ever predestinated to get "in Christ," they are predestinated to other things *after* they are "in Christ."

It's really sad that such great verses on eternal security have been stolen by the Calvinists to teach false doctrine. Verses on predestination and election are wonderful verses to show that a believer is already guaranteed a place in Heaven. Once you are predestinated, there's no going back. Once again you'd have to find a way to undo what God has done, and there is no Scripture on how to undo the corporate predestination in Christ.

Chapter Thirteen

Step Twelve: Amputate Yourself from the Body of Christ.

"So we, being many, are one body in Christ..."

Romans 12:5

Before the cross, Jesus said that we were so secure that we were held fast in the hands of God and Christ. After the cross, we are so secure that spiritually we aren't merely in Christ's hands; if anything, *we're part of Christ's hands.*

Imagine a giant extension cord reaching from Heaven all the way down to Earth. The end of this cord turns into a giant surge protector with many outlets. When a person gets saved they plug into this cord. Every Christian is plugged into this cord, and they are all attached to each other and to Christ. They are all one "in Christ."

This is something on a spiritual level that we'll never quite fully understand this side of eternity, if ever. Somehow when a man is saved, and has the Holy Spirit living inside of him (which we'll look at in the next chapter), he is attached to Christ spiritually and is part of Him spiritually. We're all one body in Christ, attached to each other and part of Christ Himself, on a spiritual level.

This isn't pantheism or some sort of spooky cult teaching. God is still God and the Trinity is still the Trinity. We do not become God or gods in eternity in any way, shape, or form.

However, being "in Christ" isn't merely agreeing with others on an intellectual basis about the doctrine of salvation. There's an actual literal – but spiritual – connection between all Christians with each other and Christ. This connection is so strong that Christ said that we are part of Him in a similar way to how He is part of God the Father, and that even though our bodies are on this Earth that we are *already* spiritually seated in heavenly places.

John 17:11, 21-23, "And now I am no more in the world, but these are in the world, and I come to thee. Holy Father, keep through thine own name those whom thou hast given me, that they may be one, as we are.
21) That they all may be one; as thou, Father, art in me, and I in thee, that they also may be one in us: that the world may believe that thou hast sent me.
22) And the glory which thou gavest me I have given them; that they may be one, even as we are one:
23) I in them, and thou in me, that they may be made perfect in one; and that the world may know that thou hast sent me, and hast loved them, as thou hast loved me."

Eph. 2:6, "And hath raised us up together, and made us sit together in heavenly places in Christ Jesus:"

John 6:53-57, 63, "Then Jesus said unto them, Verily, verily, I say unto you, Except ye eat the flesh of the Son of man, and drink his blood, ye have no life in you.

54) Whoso eateth my flesh, and drinketh my blood, hath eternal life; and I will raise him up at the last day.

55) For my flesh is meat indeed, and my blood is drink indeed.

56) He that eateth my flesh, and drinketh my blood, dwelleth in me, and I in him.

57) As the living Father hath sent me, and I live by the Father: so he that eateth me, even he shall live by me.

63) It is the spirit that quickeneth; the flesh profiteth nothing: the words that I speak unto you, they are spirit, and they are life."

Christ said that we need to eat His flesh and drink His blood to have eternal life. The Catholic Church, while choosing to spiritualize and allegorize the entire book of Revelation, decided to spastically take this verse to be physical. Christ meant what He said here *literally*, but that doesn't mean He meant it *physically*. Verse sixty-three shows that Christ meant what He said on a spiritual level, and unless Jesus is actually biting chunks of flesh off God the Father, verse fifty-seven reinforces that. The idea behind this is speaking about the body of Christ that would be formed after the cross, and how Christ lived off of the Father and was part of the Father, so in a spiritual manner we are part of Christ and live off of Him.

This is a spiritual organism called "the body of Christ." When an individual trusts Christ, they are spiritually baptized by the Holy Spirit "into Christ" and become part of this spiritual body. This baptism is spiritual; it has nothing to do with water.

Eph. 2:18, "For through him we both have <u>access by one Spirit</u> unto the Father."

I Cor. 6:17, "But <u>he that is joined unto the Lord is one spirit.</u>"

I Cor. 12:12-13, "For as the body is one, and hath many members, and all the members of that one body, being many, are <u>one body: so also is Christ.</u>"
13) For <u>by one Spirit are we all baptized into one body</u>, whether we be Jews or Gentiles, whether we be bond or free; and have been all made to <u>drink into one Spirit.</u>"

Gal. 3:27-28, "For as many of you as have been <u>baptized into Christ</u> have put on Christ.
28) There is neither Jew nor Greek, there is neither bond nor free, there is neither male nor female: for <u>ye are all one in Christ Jesus.</u>"

Rom. 6:3-4, "Know ye not, that so many of us as were baptized <u>into Jesus Christ</u> were baptized into his death?

4) Therefore we <u>are buried with him by</u> baptism into death: that like as Christ was raised up from the dead by the glory of the Father, even so we also should walk in newness of life."

Eph. 2:16, "And that he might reconcile both unto God <u>in one body by the cross</u>, having slain the enmity thereby:"

Many things happened on the cross that are not apparent to the naked eye. It was more than a Man suffering physically, there were spiritual things going as well. In the time that Christ was on the cross, on a spiritual level He paid for the sins of all time. The law was ended and the spiritual body of Christ was formed by the cross as well. When a person is saved, on a spiritual level they are baptized into His death. By the cross and what happened on it, a Christian is connected forever to Jesus Christ by spiritual baptism.

It is of the utmost importance that one remembers that these things are on a spiritual level! As the Catholic tries to make eating Christ's flesh physical, so the Campbellite tries to make the spiritual baptism a water one. The Bible says *"...by <u>one Spirit</u> are we all baptized into one body..."*

There's nothing physical about it; it's a spiritual union.

This one body is also called "the church."

Col. 1:24, "Who now rejoice in my sufferings for you, and fill up that which is behind of the afflictions

of Christ in my flesh for <u>his body's sake, which is the</u>
<u>church:</u>"

Eph. 1:22-23, "And hath put all things under his
feet, and gave him to be the head over all things to
<u>the church,</u>
23) Which<u> is his body</u>, the fulness of him that
filleth all in all."

The one body of Christ is the one true church.
There's no such thing as "the one true church" based
upon a label on a sign, contrary to the belief of the
Church of Christ, Catholic Church, and even some
Baptist churches that have sadly mistaken the rich history
of the Baptist denomination as a proof text for doctrine.
The true church has nothing to do with where you go to
worship, it is what you are. If you are saved you are part
of the one true church, and it is a spiritual church just like
the body of Christ is a spiritual body.

This, of course, isn't a support for the ecumenical
movement or the ideas that come from the teaching that
because we're all one church, we don't actually need to
belong to a local church. The local church is a very
strong doctrine in the Bible as well; local churches are
spoken of all throughout the New Testament. Paul made
it his mission to start local churches and plant pastors
such as Timothy and Titus in them. God set up the local
church system to create a localized place of unity,
accountability, encouragement, evangelism, ministry, and
worship for believers. To forsake it would be imbalanced,
unbiblical, and a sin. (I Tim. 3:15, Eph. 4:11-12, Heb.
10:25; 13:7, 17, 24)

This church and body is also Christ's bride:

Eph. 5:30-32, "For <u>we are members of his body, of his flesh, and of his bones.</u>
31) For this cause shall a man leave his father and mother, and shall be joined unto his wife, and they two shall be one flesh.
32) This is a great mystery: but <u>I speak concerning Christ and the church.</u>"

So what you have when you put all these passages together is that being "in Christ" is the same as being "in the body," which is also being "in the church," which is also being "in the bride." Understanding this Bible truth is very important, and it shatters the false doctrine of many *elitists* who would try to claim a superior position in their denomination or belief system.

Suffice it to say, we are connected to Christ in a spiritual way that is very real and extremely powerful. Without changing who He is as God and who we are as believers, we are one with Jesus Christ and part of His spiritual body.

To lose your salvation, you'd have to find a way to undo that; you'd have to figure out how to amputate yourself from the body of Christ.

Chapter Fourteen

Step Thirteen: Evict the Holy Spirit.

"Hereby know we that we dwell in him, and he in us, because he hath given us of his Spirit."

I John 4:13

Have you ever hired or met a process server? Much of the time they are ex-military, wear bullet proof vests, carry a pistol, and have a lot of stories they could tell you. In one such story, a landlord was having an extremely difficult time in getting a tenant served. He couldn't get her out of his house until he got a court order, but he couldn't get a court order until he found her.

Enter the process server with the gun and the street smarts. The man would park down the road and wait for her to show up in her pink high heels and faded Grand Am. It was easier said than done. She had a way of eluding people by sleeping at a friend's place, or having a knack for only coming home when no one was around.

However, on a midnight stakeout he finally caught her. He followed her to the local gas station and as soon as she parked he pulled up behind her and blocked her escape route. "You been served," he said as he tossed the papers onto the hood of her car.

What does that have to do with anything? Well, if you're going lose your salvation you're going to need to hire a process server that was better than he was, because you're going to need to evict the Holy Spirit.

What Christian doesn't wonder what it would have been like to walk with Christ? How wonderful it must have been to watch Him heal people and perform miracles! In spite of all that, Christ said it was more important that He leave so that the Holy Spirit would come down and indwell the believers.

John 14:6, "And I will pray the Father, and he shall give you another Comforter, that he may abide with you for ever;"

As wonderful as it must have been to have seen Christ, the sad reality for believers in that day was that Jesus couldn't be everywhere at once. Many of the people who met Jesus only had the memories of their experience to live off of when He wasn't there. However, when Christ ascended to Heaven, the Holy Spirit indwelt all the believers and the body of Christ was formed (it *may* have been formed before the Ascension as well). Led by the indwelling Holy Spirit, the apostles penned the New Testament, and as Peter said, made something more certain than any experience, even the experience of having witnessed the Transfiguration first-hand.

II Peter 1:16-19, "For we have not followed cunningly devised fables, when we made known unto you the power and coming of our Lord Jesus Christ, but <u>were eyewitnesses of his majesty.</u>

17) For he received from God the Father honour and glory, when there came such a voice to him from the excellent glory, <u>This is my beloved Son, in whom I am well pleased.</u>

18) And this voice which came from heaven we heard, <u>when we were with him in the holy mount.</u>

19) We <u>have also a more sure word of prophecy;</u> whereunto ye do well that ye take heed, as unto a light that shineth in a dark place, until the day dawn, and the day star arise in your hearts:"

In the person of the Holy Spirit, God now lives in us and is with us anywhere and everywhere we go. While it is true that God has always been omnipresent, and in the Old Testament the Spirit came upon people and occasionally went in them, before the cross there was no such thing as the body of Christ and not *every* believer had the Spirit of God living in him. Now the Bible says that if a man doesn't have the Spirit of Christ he doesn't have Christ at all – there is no middle ground. You can't be saved without having the Holy Spirit inside of you; the Holy Spirit is not something that is acquired by some second act of grace.

Rom. 8:9, "But ye are not in the flesh, but in the Spirit, if so be that the Spirit of God dwell in you. Now <u>if any man have not the Spirit of Christ, he is none of his.</u>"

Understanding that we now have the Holy Spirit inside of us, hiding from God has never been harder (as if it was really possible before). In everything we do and see we involve God because the Holy Spirit is inside of us.

Living in sin grieves the Spirit of God; He is a person with real feelings. He is not some *inanimate* force of God or nature; He is the third member of the Godhead and lives in the bodies of all saved people. Everything we do, we drag Him into it whether it is good or bad.

Eph. 4:30, "And <u>grieve not the holy Spirit of God</u>, whereby <u>ye are sealed</u> unto the day of redemption."

Notice in that verse that it states that we are "sealed" by the Holy Spirit unto the "day of redemption." This day of redemption is the Rapture. Our souls are sealed unto the day that Christ either resurrects our dead bodies or changes us and takes us home.

When a person buys a house and they are serious about the offer they make to purchase it, they put down "earnest money." That earnest money belongs to the seller if the seller accepts the offer, that way if the buyer backs out the seller at least has the earnest money to keep. God said He'd take our bodies and change them one day, removing the sin nature and making us like Christ. Besides the many other reasons the Holy Spirit indwells us, He's inside of us to show us that God means business.

Eph. 1:13-14, "In whom ye also trusted, after that ye heard the word of truth, the gospel of your salvation: in whom also after that ye believed, <u>ye were sealed with that holy Spirit of promise</u>,
14) <u>Which is the earnest of our inheritance</u> until the redemption of the purchased possession, unto the praise of his glory."

We are sealed with the Holy Spirit inside of us unto the day of redemption. It doesn't say that we are sealed unto the day we commit some heinous sin or fail to continue to work out our salvation – we are sealed forever. Those who teach one can lose his salvation fail *every time* to find a way to reconcile this. How can someone be sealed with the Holy Spirit and go to Hell? Does the Holy Spirit go to Hell with him and suffer with him? Of course not!

A child of God cannot lose his salvation; to do so you'd actually have to serve the Holy Spirit with an eviction notice. Ask any landlord: it's hard enough to get flesh and blood people evicted from your place let alone God Himself.

Chapter Fifteen

Step Fourteen: Alter the Genetic Material of Your Spirit.

*"Whosoever believeth that Jesus is the Christ
is born of God..."*

I John 5:1

The strongest scientific case against abortion is the fact that at the moment of conception that baby has all the DNA he's going to need for the rest of his life; it's only a matter of growing into it.

On a spiritual level, nothing is different for a child of God either. When a man trusts Christ, he is born again into the family of God and his spiritual DNA is forever changed.

I Peter 1:23, "Being born again, not of corruptible seed, but of incorruptible, by the word of God, which liveth and abideth for ever."

II Cor. 5:17, "Therefore if any man be in Christ, he is a new creature: old things are passed away; behold, all things are become new."

The same word of God that spoke the world into existence and brought Lazarus back to life is the same word of God that forever changes a man's spirit after salvation. We are new creatures in Christ.

God told Adam and Eve in the garden that the day in which they ate of the tree they would die (Gen. 2:17). Because they didn't fall over dead at that moment, we understand that it was their spirits that died.

When a baby is born physically, he is born with a live spirit. The body, soul, and spirit are all alive. The consequences of sin is death, and though his body is born with a sin nature, that baby's spirit has not yet experienced the consequences of sin. At the time in which they understand sin and begin to grasp the accountability of their actions, that spirit inside of them dies. They have reached the age of accountability. Christ's righteousness has not been imputed to them, but neither have their sins: they are "safe" (II Sam. 12:23).

Rom. 7:9, "For I was alive without the law once: but when the commandment came, sin revived, and I died."

Rom. 5:13, "(For until the law sin was in the world: but sin is not imputed when there is no law."

God is not in the business of sending babies to Hell who couldn't pray for forgiveness if they wanted to. In John Calvin's system, all babies who died were part of the elect (very convenient). It is very common for children growing up in a church to want to get saved, but because they do not fully understand what they are doing, *they can't*. God isn't going let that little one perish who couldn't accept Christ because he lacked the understanding and maturity.

Paul states that there was a time once in which he was alive, and then something happened, and then he was dead. Considering the fact that he was writing this, it's safe to assume he was talking about his spirit dying in the past, not his body.

At the moment of salvation, that spirit comes back to life again.

John 3:6-7, "That which is born of the flesh is flesh; and that which is born of the Spirit is spirit.
7) Marvel not that I said unto thee, Ye must be born again."

Eph. 2:1, 5, "And you hath he quickened, who were dead in trespasses and sins;
5) Even when we were dead in sins, hath quickened us together with Christ, (by grace ye are saved;)"

To quicken is to make alive. The spirit inside of a man isn't merely made alive again; it is reborn. It now responds and understands the things of God and relates with the Holy Spirit that also dwells inside the believer. Before salvation a lost man may intellectually grasp some of the teachings of the Bible, but his dead spirit does not relate to the Spirit of God.

I Cor. 2:14, "But the natural man receiveth not the things of the Spirit of God: for they are foolishness *unto him: neither can he know them, <u>because they</u> <u>are spiritually discerned.</u>"*

As was already discussed in chapter eleven, when we are adopted into God's family at salvation we are made sons of God. However, being born again into the family of God has to do with our spiritual makeup; it is who we are on a spiritual level that is just as literal and real as who we are on a physical level.

Biologically, when you are born, nothing can be changed about that. You may not like your parents, you may change your name and disown them, but genetically you will always be the child of your father. There's nothing different about it on a spiritual level either, or God wouldn't have called it being **"born again"** by **"incorruptible seed"** which **"liveth and abideth for ever"** (I Peter 1:23).

You can't change your spiritual DNA any more than you can change your physical DNA. Once a child of God, always a child of God.

Chapter Sixteen
Step Fifteen: Un-circumcise Your Soul.

"The soul that sinneth, it shall die..."

Ezekiel 18:20

Circumcision was part of the Old Covenant between God and the nation of Israel; the concept is all over the Old Testament. God says that when a person is saved in the Church Age that person is "spiritually circumcised" (Col. 2:11-13). So what is the point of this spiritual circumcision and what does it have to do with eternal security?

Spiritual circumcision is one of the strongest pillars of the doctrine of eternal security.

I John 3:9, "__Whosoever is born of God doth not__ __commit sin__; for his seed remaineth in him: and he __cannot sin__, because he is born of God."

There are a lot of things that verse *doesn't* say and one very clear thing it *does* say. That verse doesn't say that a Christian should not sin, that he won't sin as much, that he won't sin willfully or even that he must remain sinless to stay saved. That verse is written in extremely clear English and twice it says that a Christian doesn't commit sin and that *he can't sin. As in he doesn't have the ability to sin.*

Rom. 7:15-20, 24, "For that which I do I allow not: for what I would, that do I not; but what I hate, that do I.

16) If then I do that which I would not, I consent unto the law that it is good.

17) Now then <u>it is no more I that do it, but sin that dwelleth in me.</u>

18) For I know that <u>in me (that is, in my flesh,)</u> dwelleth no good thing: for to will is present with me; but how to perform that which is good I find not.

19) For the good that I would I do not: but the evil which I would not, that I do.

20) <u>Now if I do that I would not, it is no more I that do it, but sin that dwelleth in me.</u>

24) O wretched man that I am! who shall deliver me from <u>the body of this death?</u>"

This is the passage that describes the battle between the new nature and the old nature better than any other. Reading it, Paul seems like a schizophrenic. In verses fifteen and sixteen we see that sometimes a Christian does things he shouldn't and doesn't want to. It's called sin, we hate it when we do it, and we do in fact do it.

Or do we? Remember I John says that not only do we no longer sin after being born again but that we also lack the ability to sin. Does I John contradict Romans 7?

Not at all: look at verses seventeen and twenty. Paul says that when he sins, it's actually not him sinning – it's "sin within him" that is doing the sinning. In verse eighteen Paul explains that the "in him" that he's talking about is his *flesh*. In verse twenty-four he clarifies that even further by telling us that he's speaking about his body.

Within the body of every Christian and lost person lies the old, carnal, sin nature. This old nature puts self first and occasionally others second. It wants *nothing* to do with the God of the Bible. This old nature breeds sin, and it's never satisfied. Like a shark that grows to fit the size of its environment, so the unchecked old nature will let sin grow as much as possible. Anger begets rage, lust begets perversion, and laziness begets poverty.

A person is like a hard boiled egg: you have the shell on the outside, the white on the inside, and inside of that you have the yolk. The shell is the body, the white is the soul, and the yolk is the spirit. When you put Romans 7 together with I John 3:9 you understand that a Christian's body does all the sinning after salvation, but the rest of him, his soul and spirit, are no longer capable of sinning.

Heb. 10:14, "For by one offering <u>he hath perfected for ever</u> them that are <u>sanctified.</u>"

To sanctify is to "set apart." Christians are *sanctified* at the moment of salvation and are made perfect for ever. The next time someone tries to talk you out of your salvation, tell them the Bible says you're perfect and that you can't sin even if you wanted to.

Obviously, that's only half of the story. We sin all the time with our bodies. There's still 1/3 of a Christian's trichotomy (body, soul, spirit) that is far from being perfect, and we have to deal with it every day. Whether it's our thoughts on the inside or what we say on the outside, we sin every day. We are held accountable on this Earth for our sins by God in many different ways, and the only sane thing a Christian can do when he realizes he's sinned is judge himself and ask for God's forgiveness and mercy (I Cor. 11:31, I John 1:8-10).

Do you see the importance of rightly dividing the word? In I John 1:10 it says that if we claim we have no sin we make God a liar, but in I John 3:9 the Bible clearly states that we in fact do not ever sin. The difference is found in rightly dividing the word of truth. Our bodies sin, our souls and spirits do not.

How is such a thing possible?

By the operation of God.

Heb. 4:12, "For the word of God is quick, and powerful, and sharper than any twoedged sword, piercing even to _the dividing asunder of soul and spirit_, and of the _joints and marrow_, and is a discerner of the thoughts and intents of the heart."

Col. 2:11-13, "In whom also _ye are circumcised with the circumcision made without hands_, in _putting off the body_ of the sins of the flesh by the circumcision of Christ:

12) Buried with him in baptism, wherein also ye are risen with him through the faith of the operation of God, who hath raised him from the dead.

13) And you, being dead in your sins and the uncircumcision of your flesh, <u>hath he quickened together with him</u>, having forgiven you all trespasses;"

Do you ever remember reading about "the soul that sinneth" in the Old Testament? Or when it said that "if any soul toucheth..." The reason God said that all the time in the Old Testament was because before a person is saved their soul can sin. While it is true that the word soul can be interchanged for a person in general, the Bible isn't that simple and there's no coincidence to the fact that God stops using that term in the New Testament.

Souls do sin, and they do die, and when they die they go to the Lake of Fire forever. This is why God calls it "the second death" in Revelation; it follows the most obvious death: the death of the body. A man's spirit dies at the age of accountability, his body dies when his spirit leaves him (James 2:26), and his soul dies following the Great White Throne Judgment in Revelation 20.

In Hebrews we see that there is a division that happens at salvation. It speaks of the joints and marrow being divided away from the soul and the spirit. The joints and marrow aren't divided from each other, so obviously the soul and the spirit aren't either. The body is the joints and the marrow, and it is cut away from your soul and spirit.

In Colossians, we read of the "operation of God" in which a Christian is circumcised by a circumcision that is made "without hands." Verse eleven states that this operation puts off "the body of sins of the flesh." Once the body is cut away from the soul and spirit, the Holy Spirit indwells that man and his spirit is born again. Everything else discussed in this book falls into place as well, from being declared just in Heaven to being adopted and declared a son and joined to the spiritual body of Christ.

To make sure that we don't mess up everything that God has done for us, He performs a spiritual operation on us that forever separates the spirit and soul from the body. Now when a Christian sins, while it affects his body (1/3 of him) and therefore his personal relationship with God on this Earth, it does not affect his eternal condition. The sin no longer touches his soul or spirit. His soul has been cleansed by the blood of Christ and is forever protected from the ravaging consequences of sin that the body, which while still having the sin nature, is guaranteed to commit. Having established a hedge or separation to protect the spiritual side of the Christian, God promises to one day save that rotten body and predestinates the Christian to receive a glorified body that is forever free of the sin nature.

Good luck trying to undo that!

Chapter Seventeen

Ten Things a Christian Really Can Lose.

"...Take from him the pound, and give it to him that hath ten pounds."

Luke 19:24

It should be abundantly clear by this point that a Christian can not lose his salvation. The first and primary argument against a Christian being "once saved and always saved" is that a believer can go out and *"do anything he wants"* once he's saved and he'll be okay. Nothing could be further from the truth. While God isn't going to go back on His promise and throw a Christian in Hell, a rebellious child of God will still have to bear the consequences of a wasted life in time and eternity.

This is what a rebellious child of God stands to lose:

1. Joy.

Rev. 2:4, "Nevertheless I have somewhat against thee, because <u>thou hast left thy first love.</u>"

Living a life focused on self won't make a lost man happy in the long run, and it certainly won't for a saved man. That saved man has the Holy Spirit of God in him all the while he is living his life in sin. How sad to think of a man who had all the potential in the world to live for Christ, later on in life wishing he had a second chance. A Christian who only lives his life for himself will always find himself, at some point, disappointed and sorrowful for doing so.

2. Rewards.

II John 1:8, "Look to yourselves, that we <u>lose not those things</u> which we have wrought, <u>but that we receive a full reward.</u>"

The Bible is very clear that Christians get rewards in Heaven based upon Christian service in their life. The time in which Christians are rewarded is called the Judgment Seat of Christ, and it follows the Rapture of the Church. In I Corinthians 3 it speaks of Christians being rewarded with gold, silver, and precious stones. Other passages speak of five crowns that the believer can receive as well.

The truth is, no one has received a single reward as of yet. Those rewards will be given out at a future date. II John 1:8, along with the parable of the pounds in Luke 19, teach us that it is possible for Christians to lose these rewards. You could live your whole life for Christ and then blow it at the very end, destroying your testimony as many preachers have, and watch your whole life go up in smoke at the Judgment Seat of Christ.

3. Millennial Reign.

II Tim. 2:12-13, "If we suffer, <u>we shall also reign</u> with him: <u>if we deny him, he also will deny us:</u>
13) If we believe not, yet he abideth faithful: he cannot deny himself."

Some have used verse twelve to try and prove that a Christian can be denied by Christ and lose his salvation. Verse thirteen clears that up – Christ will never deny us a home in Heaven because to do so would mean He'd have to deny Himself (we are joint-heirs with Him and in the body of Christ). However, we do stand to lose a special position following the rapture.

After the Rapture, and the Tribulation, Jesus Christ will rule the world from Jerusalem. This period of time will last one thousand years (see Revelation chapter twenty) and during it the saints will reign with Christ. God says that if you suffer for Christ now on this Earth, that you'll reign with Him later on. However, if you deny Him, he'll deny you a Millennial reign.

How sad to be living in the Millennium, and even though life will be so much better than it is now, to know in the back of your mind that because you denied Christ you're missing out on the wonderful experience of reigning with Him.

4. Testimony and Influence.

Rev. 2:5, "Remember therefore from whence thou art fallen, and repent, and do the first works; or else I *will come unto thee quickly, and <u>will remove thy candlestick out of his place</u>, except thou repent."*

The candlesticks in Revelation represented churches that were in the presence of Jesus Christ. The church that refused to repent lost the power of God on it as its candlestick was taken away.

An example of this in the Old Testament is Lot. In II Peter 2:8 we read that Lot was righteous and his soul was vexed with the wickedness that was around him on a daily basis. When it came time to leave Sodom, no one took him seriously because of the company he kept (Gen. 19:14). He refused to separate himself when he should have, and as a result he lost his testimony and any influence he had as a believer.

5. Life.

Acts 5:3-5, "But Peter said, Ananias, why hath Satan filled thine heart to lie to the Holy Ghost, and to keep back part of the price of the land?

4) Whiles it remained, was it not thine own? and after it was sold, was it not in thine own power? why hast thou conceived this thing in thine heart? thou hast not lied unto men, but unto God.

5) And Ananias hearing these words fell down, <u>and gave up the ghost:</u> and great fear came on all them that heard these things."

As God killed Ananias and Sapphira for lying in Acts 5, sometimes God just kills Christians who won't get right. We'll go into this a little more in the next chapter, but just remember you are not your own. You are bought with a price and we are left here to glorify our Saviour.

6. Health.

I Cor. 11:29-30, "For he that eateth and drinketh unworthily, <u>eateth and drinketh damnation to himself</u>, not discerning the Lord's body.
30) For <u>this cause many are weak and sickly</u> among you, and many sleep."

The "damnation" in verse twenty-nine is clarified to be temporal in verse thirty, that is, they suffer the consequences in this life, not the next. It's possible for a Christian to lose his health because of sin. In this case it's because they were taking part in the Lord's Supper with unrepentant hearts; some even died.

There's a true story about a pastor who had problem with adultery in his church. Several families were involved in "swinging," and they refused to get right. Oddly enough, they kept coming to church. The details of this story are not clear as to whether or not the pastor attempted to "church" the swingers or not, or even if he knew who they all were. One thing is clear though: the pastor began a policy of having communion every Sunday. The adulterers were there, and they took part in it every week. Within the course of a year, several of them died and eventually the problem went away.

Thankfully, God is longsuffering and merciful, but the Scriptures tell us He will suddenly destroy the stubborn and rebellious. God hates arrogance and pride. We should always try to live right for the Lord because we love him, but God wasn't kidding when He said "the fear of the Lord is the beginning of wisdom."

7. Peace.

Luke 22:62, "And Peter went out, and wept bitterly."

Peter wasn't humming *"Peace, peace, wonderful peace, coming down from…"* that night. He sat alone that night in the cold air, sobbing that he had denied his Savior. He lost his peace. Many Christians lose their peace because they've ruined their relationship with the Father. They're still saved, but sin has gotten in between them and God.

Many people ignore the clear teachings of the Bible and head down the path of life based upon their own wisdom. This is especially true when it comes to finances and child training. When they wind up in over their heads, they have no where to turn because the road behind them was paved with worldly wisdom. They have no peace because they suddenly realize that the security they had was based in man's philosophies and not the promises found in the word of God. The only cure for this is to give up everything you thought you knew and dig deep into the word of God for the truth, and then to latch hold of the promises of God with everything you've got.

8. Protection of God.

I Cor. 5:5, "To deliver such an one unto Satan for the destruction of the flesh, that the spirit may be saved in the day of the Lord Jesus."

Once again, we are reading about punishment that is dealt in this life – not the next life. In this case we have Paul recommending that a local church "deliver" a young man unto Satan for the destruction of the flesh, but that the man's spirit would still be saved.

Job is the reason why we know that terrible events in one's life don't always indicate sin in one's life. It's a terrifying thought to think of what Satan would like to do to you. He is evil incarnate, and would do everything to you that he did to Job if God let him. In fact, Satan would have done more to Job, but God limited him.

The protection of God is not something to be taken for granted. God will kill a Christian, allow a Christian to become sick, and He will also remove His hand of protection over a Christian and allow Satan to have his way with him.

9. Blessings of God.

Mal. 3:10, "Bring ye all the tithes into the storehouse, that there may be meat in mine house, and prove me now herewith, saith the LORD of hosts, if I will not open you the windows of heaven, and pour you out a blessing, that there shall not be room enough to receive it."

85

In the Old Testament God blessed people for tithing, and there's no reason to believe that in the New Testament He doesn't do the same. One can hear testimony after testimony of God's provision during hard times, and the blessings, both tangible *and intangible* that come down from God upon the believer. Those who live their lives for the Lord experience the blessings of God in their lives.

There's nothing quite as wonderful as seeing God do something special in your life. It makes a child of God feel special and uniquely loved by his Father. How sad would it be for a Christian to live his whole life for himself and never know what this is like!

10. Assurance of Salvation.

I Tim. 4:2, "Speaking lies in hypocrisy; having their conscience seared with a hot iron;"

Some people aren't confused about salvation as described in chapter one of this book. Instead, some Christians have scorned the grace of God and lived their lives in sin. When this happens, the Holy Spirit is quenched (He's still there, you just can't hear Him anymore) and the man's conscience is seared. Very often when this happens, the assurance of salvation is gone. *"How could I be saved and do..."* This isn't a matter of God taking something away from you; it's just one of the many natural consequences of sin.

As you can see, a Christian does stand to lose a lot, or miss out on some pretty wonderful things if he lives his life for himself. Paul warned the Romans to not sin that "grace may abound." God is merciful, but He's not one to be trifled with.

Chapter Eighteen

The Confusing Verse Checklist.

"Search the scriptures..."

I John 5:39

What do you do when you know what the truth is and you have plenty of Scripture to back it up, and then out of the blue someone pulls a verse on you that throws you for a loop? This final chapter isn't going to be an attempt to explain every verse in the Bible that may seem a little confusing; instead it's going to give the reader an idea of how to examine a verse that at first may seem to be contradictory to already established truths.

1. Double Take.

The first thing to do when someone shows you a tricky verse is to take a second look at it. Many of the "proof-texts" against eternal security are stretched to say something they do not. By reading the verse twice, a lot of times it explains itself very clearly. If not, take a look at the context and surrounding verses.

Example:

Gal. 5:4, "Christ is become of no effect unto you, <u>whosoever of you are justified by the law;</u> ye are <u>fallen from grace.</u>"

Being "fallen from grace" is one of the teachings of those that are anti-eternal security. They teach that you can reach a point that you "fall from grace."

This one is so simple you don't even *need* to look at the context around the verse. It's amazing that they even use this because it goes completely against what they're trying to teach to begin with. The verse explains itself: people who are justified by the law (or good works) are fallen from grace. It has nothing to do with being bad and losing your salvation; it's about someone who's decided that they are going to be justified by good works – they've fallen from grace. This happens before salvation.

What's ironic about this is that those who teach you can "lose it" say that the way you lose it is by either being too bad or not being good enough. Both teachings come from the same idea: *you* being justified by what *you* do. The verse is telling you the *exact opposite!* The truth is, if you believe you're saved by works then you never got saved to begin with.

2. Almost Persuaded.

The saddest thing in the world is when someone almost gets saved, but doesn't. It happens a lot, and there are even a few incidences of it in the Bible. Sometimes these verses are mishandled and used to teach that a saved person can lose it when in fact that person never "got it" in the first place.

Example:

Heb. 10:38-39, "Now <u>the just shall live by faith</u>: but if <u>any man draw back</u>, my soul shall have no pleasure in him.

39) But we are not of them who draw back unto perdition; <u>but of them that believe</u> to the saving of the soul."

This is another very simple passage to explain that also happens to be one of the other side's staple passages. The idea is that if you quit believing you'll lose it. However, an idea like that contradicts this passage:

I Tim. 2:13, "<u>If we believe not, yet he abideth faithful: he cannot deny himself.</u>"

Even if we stop believing in Jesus we're still saved because of all the things that happened at the point of salvation that *can't* be undone. One of those things is being placed into the body of Christ. Jesus can't deny us a home in Heaven because we're part of Him spiritually and *He can't deny Himself!*

Therefore the only possible explanation that the passage in Hebrews has to a Christian in this age is that of someone who comes close to getting saved, *but doesn't.* Like King Agrippa, trembling under the convicting power of the Holy Ghost said, *"Almost thou persuadest me to be a Christian."*

3. Dispensational Considerations.

It's becoming trendy to claim to not be a dispensationalist. One preacher who is very proud of his non-dispensational stand recently came out claiming that if you believed in the death penalty at all you should be for the mass killing of homosexuals or you're a hypocrite. The idea being the same God who said put a murderer to death also said to put a sodomite to death as well. For some reason he failed to mention that God also said to kill anyone who picked up sticks on Saturday morning to make a fire and cook his breakfast.

In this age our focus is to be on winning the lost to Christ, not trying to bring our government under a theocratic Old Testament law system (i.e. the Millennium). The truth is, everyone is a dispensationalist to some degree: they just don't know it, don't want to admit it, or they'd rather use a different word.

Regardless of how you do it, God commands students of the Bible to "rightly divide" His word (II Tim. 2:15). Call the divisions whatever you want, but the divisions must be made for there to be any sense to what you're reading.

Here's a couple examples:

Matt. 24:13, "But <u>he that shall endure unto the end</u>, the same shall be saved."

Others teach that this verse means that one of the requirements for salvation is that you remain faithful unto the end of your life. That completely ignores the fact that God said when you trust Christ you get eternal life then, not later (I John 5:12). You don't receive eternal life after death; you get it at the moment of faith.

By looking at the context of this passage, it's very clear that it's talking about people in a different age. It's talking about people during the Tribulation period right before the Second Advent. Some argue that people during the Tribulation must remain faithful to God or they lose their salvation, others say that this verse just means that if they hold out unto the end Christ will save them *physically* when He returns.

It's doesn't matter all that much either way: the point is that this verse has nothing to do with you. This verse is talking about people living in a different time period subject to different rules.

Matt. 24:44-51, "<u>Therefore be ye also ready: for in such an hour as ye think not the Son of man cometh.</u>

45 Who then is a faithful and wise servant, whom his lord hath made ruler over his household, to give them meat in due season?

46) Blessed is that servant, whom his lord when he cometh shall find so doing.

47) Verily I say unto you, That he shall make him ruler over all his goods.

48) But and if that evil servant shall say in his heart, <u>My lord delayeth his coming;</u>

49) And shall begin to smite his fellowservants, and to eat and drink with the drunken;

50) The lord of that servant shall come in a day when he looketh not for him, and in an hour that he is not aware of,

51) And shall cut him asunder, and appoint him his portion with the hypocrites: <u>there shall be weeping and gnashing of teeth.</u>"

This is another example of the same thing. Many teach that this is a person who lost his salvation. The best answer to this is, *"So what if he did? That's not a Church Age saint."*

This verse can be taught one of two ways: it's a man in the Tribulation who said he was saved and never was, or it's someone in the Tribulation losing his salvation.

Pick one.

The point is that what you are reading here *has no application* to you *doctrinally* any more than Leviticus 4:35 or Ezekiel 18:24. The most important thing to understand when studying this passage is knowing that whatever is going on here, it's not happening to a born-again child of God *before* the Rapture of the Church. Many of the tough passages that are thrown at Bible believers are ripped out of their context without any dispensational consideration being made.

When studying the Bible, one must always rightly divide it and make the distinction between different ages and how God dealt with people in different ways.

4. Temporal versus Eternal.

While living on this Earth, God deals with us as with sons. Hebrews 12 says, *"...for what son is he whom the father chasteneth not?"* It's called getting a correction from God, and it can come in many different ways. God occasionally chastises us to get us back in line. He does it for our benefit and because He loves us. Every child of God is different and He deals with us all differently.

The word "temporal" is where we get the word "temporary." While we live our lives, we are living in a temporal world, with temporal bodies, and in a temporal situation. One day it will all be fixed. While we live in this temporal condition, we may receive punishment in this life for sins we commit. However, in the eternal world we bear no punishment for sin because Christ bore it all *eternally* while on Calvary.

Many times the verses that speak of Christians being punished for their sins in this life are used to teach that we can lose it and suffer God's wrath in the next life. Which begs the question, *why then did Jesus die in the first place?*

Example:

I Cor. 3:16-17, "Know ye not that ye are the temple of God, and that the Spirit of God dwelleth in you?
17) If any man defile the temple of God, him shall God destroy; for the temple of God is holy, which temple ye are."

The false teaching here is that God will destroy a Christian by throwing him in Hell. The passage doesn't say that; in fact, the preceding verse tells us that even if a person received no rewards in Heaven for what he did here, he'd still be saved:

I Cor. 3:15, "If any man's work shall be burned, he shall suffer loss: <u>but he himself shall be saved; yet so as by fire.</u>"

So what you're looking at here is someone who did some really bad things after he was saved. God apparently tried to chastise and correct him, but this man continually defiled the temple of God. So God destroyed him. That's doesn't mean God sent him to Hell – it just means God killed him. God destroyed the temple of the Holy Ghost in this passage, not the man's soul.

So what is the temple of the Holy Ghost?

I Cor. 6:9, "<u>What? know ye not that your body is the temple of the Holy Ghost</u> which is in you, which ye have of God, and ye are not your own?"

It's your body! It is possible to defile your body with unrepentant sin and filth to the point where God will kill you.

It's ironic that people balk at the idea that God would physically kill a Christian for being bad, but believe somehow that He'll throw them in Hell. *Which is worse,* an early grave or eternal Hell? It's much more plausible that God will take a Christian home to Heaven "before his time" than the idea that God will forsake all He's promised a Christian and send him to Hell.

In I Corinthians 5 Paul advised a church to pray that an unrepentant fornicator in their midst would be delivered to Satan for the destruction of the flesh, but reminded the people that if God chose to kill the man that his spirit would still be saved.

The passages are very simple and to the point – if you defile the temple, God just might kill you, but you can never lose the gift of salvation.

Rom. 11:29, "For the gifts and calling of God are without repentance."

5. National versus Individual.

Some verses apply to groups of people losing a special blessing or position with God. These passages have been hijacked from their context to teach that an individual can lose his salvation.

Example:

Rom. 11:18-26, "Boast not against the branches. But if thou boast, thou bearest not the root, but the root thee.
19) Thou wilt say then, The branches were broken off, that I might be graffed in.
20) Well; because of unbelief they were broken off, and thou standest by faith. Be not highminded, but fear:

21) For if God spared not the natural branches, take heed lest he also spare not thee.

22) Behold therefore the goodness and severity of God: on them which fell, severity; but toward thee, goodness, if thou continue in his goodness: <u>otherwise thou also shalt be cut off.</u>

23) And they also, if they abide not still in unbelief, shall be graffed in: <u>for God is able to graff them in again.</u>

24) For if thou wert cut out of the olive tree which is wild by nature, and wert graffed contrary to nature into a good olive tree: how much more shall these, which be the natural branches, be graffed into their own olive tree?

25) <u>For I would not, brethren, that ye should be ignorant of this mystery, lest ye should be wise in your own conceits; that blindness in part is happened to Israel, until the fulness of the Gentiles be come in.</u>

26) And <u>so all Israel shall be saved:</u> as it is written, There shall come out of Sion the Deliverer, and shall turn away ungodliness from Jacob:"

One of the most important things in the Bible to understand is the nation of Israel. Israel is God's first choice, and when you read Romans 11 you'll see that as a nation she's been *partially blinded* to the truth of the Gospel. In fact, the chapter goes so far as to say they are "enemies" of the Gospel, but at the same time they are "beloved" of the Father.

This has to do with the nation of Israel as a whole. What you're reading about here with the olive branches is

God's relationship and dealings with Israel and the Gentiles. Israel rejected their Messiah multiple times during the book of Acts (and before) and eventually God "turned" from the Jew to the Gentile.

Acts 13:46, "Then Paul and Barnabas waxed bold, and said, <u>It was necessary that the word of God should first have been spoken to you:</u> but seeing ye put it from you, and judge yourselves unworthy of everlasting life, <u>lo, we turn to the Gentiles."</u>

Acts 28:25-28, "And when they agreed not among themselves, they departed, after that Paul had spoken one word, <u>Well spake the Holy Ghost by Esaias the prophet unto our fathers,</u>

26) Saying, Go unto this people, and say, Hearing ye shall hear, and shall not understand; and seeing ye shall see, and not perceive:

27) For the <u>heart of this people is waxed gross, and their ears are dull of hearing, and their eyes have they closed;</u> lest they should see with their eyes, and hear with their ears, and understand with their heart, and should be converted, and I should heal them.

28) Be it known therefore unto you, that <u>the salvation of God is sent unto the Gentiles</u>, and that they will hear it."

So you see, Paul is explaining that just like God turned from the Jews to the Gentiles, He can just as easily turn from the Gentiles back to the Jews. What you're looking at is God dealing corporately, not individually. He's dealing with nations, not individuals.

When unrepentant nations turn their backs on God, He eventually turns His back on them.

Lastly, in Romans 11:26 we understand that one day God will save all of Israel. This Israel that one day will be saved is *the same Israel* that God says is partially blind and an enemy of the Gospel! One day God will restore the nation of Israel back to a nation that loves and serves Him. This is the whole point of the Tribulation period that follows the Rapture.

6. Professors versus Possessors.

This isn't professors as in teachers; it's okay, if you teach at a local community college; God loves you too and you're not going to lose your salvation.

What this point is about is people who claim to be saved but are not. This shouldn't be any surprise: most of them you can spot without having much discernment at all. Any pastor (or hireling) that would go on a TV show and be incapable of answering simple questions about how you go to Heaven to an audience of millions is either not saved to begin with or he is a coward. *He is claiming to be something he is not.*

God talks about these people in very harsh terms. Sometimes people confuse these men with actual Christians and think God is talking about sending a child of God to Hell. Not true, of course.

Example:

II Peter 2:20-21, "For if after they have escaped the pollutions of the world through the knowledge of the Lord and Saviour Jesus Christ, they are again entangled therein, and overcome, <u>the latter end is worse with them than the beginning.</u>

21) For it had been better for them not to have known the way of righteousness, than, after they have known it, to turn from the holy commandment delivered unto them."

This passage is used to teach that if you are overcome by sin you'll lose your salvation. The list of problems with this interpretation is very long, but suffice it to say these are people who never got saved in the first place. They lived clean lives because they had a head knowledge of the Bible and Christ, but they never received Him by faith.

How do we know they're lost and were never saved to begin with?

1. They're dogs, not sheep (Vs. 22). A lost man is a dog in the Bible; a saved man is a sheep and a new creature in Christ.

2. They're "wells without water" (Vs. 17). Christians are wells with water (John 4:14).

3. They're "brute beasts," not sheep (Vs. 12).

4. They can not cease from sin (Vs. 14). A Christian can overcome sin.

5. They're "cursed children" (Vs. 14), not children of God.

6. They turned away from the holy commandment. The holy commandment is to believe on Christ in I John 3:23. They never did; they turned away from it.

7. They are servants of corruption, and even though they promise liberty to their audience, they themselves are earning the reward of unrighteousness (Vs. 19, 13).

So when you come across a verse that may look like a person can lose his salvation, it's important to consider if the person in the passage was ever truly saved in the first place.

7. Weight of Scripture.

In this book you have read scripture after scripture and promise after promise of God's eternal love and salvation for the believer. You have seen not only the promises made that if a man simply believes in Christ he will never come into condemnation without any exception given, but you've also seen some of the more complicated doctrines that intertwine with the doctrine of eternal security. From doctrines relating to the body, soul, and spirit of a believer, to eternal judicial decrees made by God at salvation, to the permanent identity we have within the spiritual body of Christ: a born-again child of God in this age can not undo everything that God has done for him *and to him* at the moment of salvation.

Those who teach you can lose your salvation are divided into two camps: cultists and sincere believers. Along with teaching you can lose it, the first group is also likely to teach other very alarming things if you really get into it. *Such as:* Jesus was a created god or He's actually Michael the Archangel, the sacrifice of Christ needs to be applied every week via a cracker, or that the Second Coming has already occurred in a spiritual non-literal manner.

In the other camp, there are good-hearted and sincere Christians who really love the Lord but have just *"missed it"* on this vital truth. If that is you, please consider on what side of the room you are standing and who is over there with you – *the guy who says Jesus is Michael.* Take a look at the Bible verses and how deep the doctrines are that you have supporting what you believe, and compare them to what you read in this book. When compared with all the other very clear promises given in the New Testament, do a couple of confusing or stretched verses here and there really teach what you think they teach? Call it what you want, brother or sister, but do you really think that God's way is for you to *not* earn your salvation before you are saved but somehow you're supposed to earn it *after you are saved?*

Lastly, if you are a new Christian or struggling with assurance, please understand that there will be times when someone might show you a verse that might be confusing and hard to understand. You can use a Bible verse to teach all sorts of things that are wrong. But what you can't do is use a hundred verses to teach something that is wrong. When verse after verse tells you that you can't lose it don't let someone else tell you otherwise.

Trust the weight of Scripture, *and always interpret that which is unclear in light of that which is clear.*

You're a child of God, an adopted son and a joint-heir with Jesus Christ. Your advocate is Christ Himself; furthermore you are kept by the power of God the Father.

You are forever and eternally accepted in the beloved as a member of the family of God, not because of anything you can ever do to earn it, but because of what He already did for you.

Don't let the Devil steal your joy.

Ecclesiastes 3:14, "I know that, whatsoever God doeth, it shall be for ever: nothing can be put to it, nor any thing taken from it: and God doeth it, that men should fear before him."

Made in the USA
Middletown, DE
11 June 2022